BE BOLD!

AND DISCOVER THE
POWER *of* PRAISE

BRILLIANT, GORGEOUS, TALENTED,
FABULOUS. WHY NOT?

BE BOLD!

AND DISCOVER THE
POWER *of* PRAISE

SUSAN MITCHELL

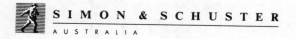
SIMON & SCHUSTER
AUSTRALIA

BRILLIANT, GORGEOUS,
TALENTED, FABULOUS.
WHY NOT?
BE BOLD AND DISCOVER
THE POWER OF PRAISE
Susan Mitchell© 2000

First published in Australia in 2000 by
Simon & Schuster (Australia) Pty Limited
20 Barcoo Street,
East Roseville NSW 2069

A Viacom Company
Sydney New York London Toronto Tokyo Singapore

National Library of Australia
Cataloguing-in-Publication Data

Mitchell, Susan, 1945– .
Be bold! and discover the power of praise.

Bibliography.
ISBN 0 7318 0495 3.

1. Praise. 2. Encouragement. 3. Interpersonal relations.
I. Title.

158.2

Set in Stempel Garamond 11pt on 14pt leading
Cover and text design by Gayna Murphy, Greendot Design
Printed in Australia by Griffin Press

10 9 8 7 6 5 4 3 2

Our deepest fear is not that we are inadequate. Our deepest fear is that we are powerful beyond measure. It is our light, not our darkness, that most frightens us.

We ask ourselves, 'Who am I to be brilliant, gorgeous, talented and fabulous?' Actually, who are you not to be? ... Your playing small does not serve the world. There's nothing enlightened about shrinking so that other people won't feel insecure around you.

And as we let our own light shine, we unconsciously give other people permission to do the same.

NELSON MANDELA

CONTENTS

THE MESSAGE IS SIMPLE,
DIRECT AND TOTALLY WITHIN
YOUR GRASP.

This book promises that once you understand and use the power of praise, not only in your life but in the lives of others, you will have tapped into something that will change yours and everyone's life for the better. Whatever your goals or dreams, what you learn in this book will make them more attainable. There is no false hype, no psychological jargon, no major buzz words. For every anecdote I tell, I know you will have your own. Through my own experiences, the people I have met and the books I have written, I have learnt to give and receive praise. So, I hope, will you. And in that giving and receiving to understand how the power of praise will make you bold. Bold enough to be the person you want to become or just bold enough to be the person you already are.

For Mitch, my father

Special thanks must go to the following people:
All the women who have generously allowed me to put them in my previous books; Tim Curnow, my literary agent; Graeme Bennett and Jan Smith, my ABC radio colleagues; Jon Attenborough, Julie Stanton, Brigitta Doyle, Karen Jennings (Aust) and Fran Cregan (USA) from Simon & Schuster; Julia Collingwood, my editor; Jane Burridge, for her comments and encouragement on an early draft; Gill Harvie and All-In-One Business Services; Maggie Tabberer, for her nurturing, her food and wine, and her dining room table; and Mary Beasley, who believes in me, always.

FOREWORD

It's more than appropriate that Susan should write this book. You see, Susan has been praised all her life. That's because she's so maddeningly good at everything (except fixing things around the house) and because she has had the good sense to be raised and only mix with people who were intelligent enough to understand the power of praise. Her father was her first and most constant giver of praise. His confidence in her knew no bounds, so Susan grew to think anything and everything was possible. She also became an outrageous show-off. We all forgive her because she is witty, wonderful and too bloody bright by half.

As my friend and mentor she spent days at my farm in the Southern Highlands, preparing and writing this book. At the time I was also struggling to complete my autobiography. We would plant ourselves at opposite ends of the giant dining room table and with heads down (and bums up) we would write. Her chapters, neatly labelled, gradually grew in piles down one side of the table to touch my space, then up and down the other side. Sandwiched between her chapters, I eventually gave up and went to my desk in the study.

But even in the midst of writing this book, she always took time to pay attention to mine as it finally found form. Her criticism, while rare, was always constructive and she never failed to add a word of praise. I found it comforting, encouraging and stimulating. Her praise made me bold. It dispelled all my fears regarding writing about my life. She constantly told me I could do it, I would do it and that it would be a great success, all of which came true. But without her encouragement to be bold, bold enough to be totally truthful, would I have found my voice, would I have written a best-seller? No.

If reading this book can change your life or the lives of those around you, just a fraction of what Susan's praise did for me, then you will be blessed and those around you will be blessed.

Like ripples in the pond, the power of praise spreads out to touch both those who give it and those who receive it. And it's wonderful, bloody wonderful. Just like Susan.

Maggie Tabberer

1

BOLD OR BOLDER?

Would you like to be able to take your life by the throat and give it a good shake? Or at least a bit of a tickle?

Would you like to believe that whatever fate decrees, you will be able to act with imagination, courage and strength? Or at least be less wimpish?

Would you like at whatever stage of your life you are in to feel that you have so far given it all a good whirl? Or just a bit of rock 'n' roll? Or are you waiting to win the Lotto? Or strike gold before you can really live?

Ask yourself this question. Now. If you were on a plane and it started to go into a terminal dive what would you regret not having done or achieved in your life? Or not even attempted.

Write these things down. Now. Go on. Do it. Just off the top of your head. Look at your list. Cross out 'win the lotto' or anything else that relies on luck. Focus on those things that you could attain.

Would you like, today, to take that leap, to make those first tentative steps towards beginning whatever it is you dream you would like to achieve?

Would you like, in short, to be bold? Or bolder?

Even as you are saying yes, I know you feel the shadow. The shadow of fear, of doubt, the shadow of all the excuses that you make to yourself for why your life hasn't or isn't going the way you had hoped. Too old, too young, too many family responsibilities, not enough money, too tired, too timid, too stressed, too fat, wrong job, wrong partner ... or perhaps in truth just too lazy, too bored or too plain scared to take a risk and make a change. Yes, yes you cry, enough. Of course I would like to be bold, bold enough not to care if in trying I look foolish and more importantly having tried and failed, to find the courage to try again.

What is the key, the trigger, that will be the catalyst for you to begin the process now? What will dispel the shadow that falls between the desire to act and whatever it is that stops you? This book has the answer and the method whereby you can begin to achieve your goals and fulfil your potential. Or at least it has some suggestions to get you started.

> OF COURSE I WOULD LIKE TO BE BOLD, BOLD ENOUGH NOT TO CARE IF IN TRYING I LOOK FOOLISH AND MORE IMPORTANTLY HAVING TRIED AND FAILED, TO FIND THE COURAGE TO TRY AGAIN.
> WHAT IS THE KEY, THE TRIGGER, THAT WILL BE THE CATALYST FOR YOU TO BEGIN THE PROCESS NOW?

Think now, recall a specific occasion when someone you respected or cared about in your childhood gave you genuine praise for something you had done. It could be anything at all. A drawing, a game of sport, reading aloud, writing a story, caring for a sick pet or singing a song.

Focus on this incident, visualise the person who is giving you this praise. Recognise that this is a 'golden nugget' that you have tucked away for when times are tough and you are feeling low.

See them say it, hear them say it, look at their face. Focus on it. How does this memory make you feel? Is it like sunshine on your face? Like the comforting warmth of an open fire on a winter's night? Let the warm flush, the rosy glow of confidence flow through you. This feeling, I believe, is the trigger;

the key to the beginning of boldness. You describe it. What is the basis of this feeling? Simple praise. No hype, no psycho-babble, no false flattery, just good old-fashioned genuine praise. You could call it recognition or appreciation, or encouragement, or enthusiasm. The truth is that most of us are mean with it; we do not know how to give it generously or receive it gracefully. Yet we all spend our lives craving it. From the first moment we can remember we run and hop and skip and dance and sing so someone will clap and say 'clever boy or girl'. And then as we get older we try desperately to be in the best football or tennis team, the school choir or the school play. And if we achieve one of these ambitions, the praise that follows is the real prize. And even if it isn't lavish we are happy to accept crumbs from the high table. We are all hungry for praise or recognition or encouragement for our efforts. And why not?

As a child, a parent, a worker, an employer, a lover, a friend, a man, a woman, we all need to discover the empowerment of praise in all its shapes and forms. I know that 'empowerment' is a currently trendy term so perhaps 'energy' is a less pretentious word but I do believe that only when we learn how to use the energy or the power of praise, will we be bold. Bold enough to begin whatever it is we dream we can be or become. Praise enriches. It leads you to act.

We all stand on the threshold of boldness. At least we want to believe so. Read this book and open the door. That's my theory and I'm sticking to it. I have never written a book like this before. In fact I can hardly believe I am writing it. So why am I? Why waste the time, the effort and the paper? Clearly because I believe in it. Totally.

In *Tomorrow is Now*, Eleanor Roosevelt's last book, published after her death in 1963, she wrote:

> *'there is no more liberating, no more exhilarating experience than to determine one's position, state it bravely and then act BOLDLY.'*

2

MY FATHER'S GIFT

It all started in 1992 when, taking leave from a full-time job as a university lecturer, I presented my own daily radio program on the ABC. I was fulfilling a childhood dream. When I was ten years old a school friend had told me about a place in the city called the Coca Cola Bottlers Club where they ran a quiz show that was broadcast live over the radio. Even though I was not allowed to go to the city on my own, my friend and I made up cover stories about playing at each other's houses and boldly caught the tram into the city. For me the excitement wasn't so much the winning of a few prizes but the excitement of auditioning and possibly winning the role of Junior Announcer for the Coca Cola Bottlers Club. I stood in my little white bobby socks reading a commercial about the joys of my favourite soft drink in front of a huge microphone. Ever since I have longed to be on the radio. When I rang my father to come and pick us up he said, 'You know there will be hell to pay when you get home'. My only reply was, 'It was worth it'.

So finally many years later, there I was in front of a microphone every morning, on the radio talking to the entire State. In the middle of the panic and excitement of the early weeks, one thing stood out. Every time I interviewed an author of a 'self-help' book, the station switchboard went wild. For days and sometimes weeks after the interview, the calls kept coming. And coming. They all asked the same question, 'Where can I get that book on how to be happy, or wealthy, or thin, or successful, or cholesterol free, or cancer free, or more assertive, etc.'. It seemed the public could not get enough of these books. Why? Well none of it is probably surprising after the excesses of the 1980s where the false gods of greed and conspicuous consumerism were exposed. The so-called 'heroes' had all fallen from grace and people felt lost and confused. All the research in the 1990s points to the fact that people feel they can no longer trust the established organisations of church and state. They don't trust their religious or political leaders. In fact they actively loathe most of their politicians. The family as they have known it is changing, and marriage is no longer generally considered a sacred institution. All the traditional structures that have served as safety nets are transforming themselves into new and more diverse forms. Regardless of whether we believe in a god or a higher power, whether we follow the teachings of a church or a guru, or the dictates of our class or caste, or the influence of our school or parents, or leave it all up to astrology, numerology or crystals, we all seem to have come to one conclusion: being born is like getting a ticket in the lottery of life. We are assigned a certain set of numbers and we spend the rest of our lives trying to work out why these numbers, why this combination, and what to do with them in order to win a prize.

At the end of the twentieth century there was an all-pervasive belief that it is up to each individual to make the most of the numbers that she or he has drawn. The 1990s emerged as the decade of self-analysis, self-help and self-responsibility. Hence the popularity of the genre that has been named 'self-help' books.

We live in a time of great uncertainty and deep insecurity, both in our personal and professional lives. Somehow the excitement, creativity and vitality that followed the end of the Second World War has not translated itself into the world that we hoped we would be able to create.

We know that we are on the brink of the global revolution; a technological revolution as big as, if not bigger than, the industrial revolution and it will flow into all aspects of our work and our lives. Huge changes bring great insecurities but also great opportunities. Will we embrace them or deny them? The answer will probably depend on our level of boldness.

In 1992 as 'self-help' book after 'self-help' book crossed my desk and my microphone, each one upgrading the hyperbole of their claims, I became increasingly sceptical. Each book seemed to create a new set of jargon, a new list of impossible demands, a new, more grandiose, life-plan.

THERE HAD TO BE A BOOK THAT COULD CUT THROUGH THE JARGON AND THE HYPE AND THE PHONEY SLOGANS. A BOOK THAT TAPPED INTO KNOWLEDGE WE ALREADY POSSESS.

I kept thinking that while the needs of millions of people can't be wrong, there had to be a book that could cut through the jargon and the hype and the phoney slogans. A book that did not require an evangelical conversion. A book that tapped into knowledge we already possess. A book that would give the reader a pathway to energy, hope and self-esteem in simple, clear language.

All of these things I kept saying, ranting even, to the producers of my radio program. 'Well go on then, smarty pants, write it', was their only reply. And that soon shut me up. As the appetite for these books grew to seemingly insatiable proportions, my producers' challenge continued to nag away at the back of my mind. This challenge was then reinforced by a total stranger who stopped me when I was shopping in a department store. Fixing me with the steely eye of the Ancient Mariner she praised my books and then said, 'We know what all the people in your books stand for, Susan, but what about you? When are you going to write about your own beliefs? We want to know what you think'. I laughed in response but her words haunted me. I have always believed that you should listen to your readers, but to write such a book was just too hard.

Then, in the middle of my second month of trying to perfect the techniques of a good broadcaster, my father died. He was old and in no pain. But I was suddenly an orphan. The death of a parent is always more traumatic than we ever expect. When my mother had died five years previously, I was catapulted into the realisation that one of the two people who had always loved me, unconditionally, was gone. Even though she had been sick for most of my life and since I was 12 I had been afraid she would die, it was a shock. I coped by pouring my love and energy into ensuring that my father was not lonely. He had always been my rock. This was the man who had dragged himself out of bed at 4 a.m. to pick me and my girlfriends up from late night dances. No request was too big or too small. Although no saint himself, nor did he view me in any idealised way, he simply conveyed a firm belief that I would succeed in whatever I tried. If I failed, his reply was always the same, 'Never mind my darling, I know you did your best'. My earliest memories are all of my father — warm, smiling, confident. I had always believed that whatever happened to me, I would cope because he had convinced me that I was capable of dealing with anything that fate or my own actions thrust upon me. During my rebellious years when I was displaying the usual obnoxious behaviour of pubescent girls, he would simply take me aside and say, 'I wish you didn't feel you had to speak or act like that. I don't think it's worthy of you. I would do anything for you, there's no need to carry on in that manner'.

As I sat in the studio the morning after his death, having insisted the show must go on, I knew my producers were waiting for me to crack. They kept assuring me that I could leave at any time, and that no-one would think less of me. But I wanted to do the program with courage and dignity. I wanted to do it for my father. My grieving I knew would come later, but I did feel very strange. I took a deep breath and pressed the microphone button. His voice, still with me inside my head, said, 'I know you can do this, my girl'. And of course I did. The gift my father gave me was praise. Genuine, loving, sustaining praise. And it was this gift that gave me the strength, the courage, the boldness not to falter.

In the months that followed his death, I began slowly to realise that this is the greatest gift a parent can give to a child. How often do you hear men and women admitting that one or both of their parents never really gave them that kind of praise? And then it seems to inevitably follow that whatever they are given by others is never enough. How often do you witness grown-up children, overwhelmed with grief after the death of parents saying, 'I never told them how much I admired them or loved them. I never gave them the praise they deserved'? Or if their relationship with their parents had been difficult, they regretted that they had never said, 'I know we had our problems and I wished that we could have resolved them better than we did. But you should know that I believe you always tried, in your own way, to do your best'.

In contrast to my father's example of giving praise spontaneously and generously was the daily behaviour of the manager of the radio station. Even when our program's ratings reached new heights, he could not give us genuine praise. He knew he should make an effort, but praise always stuck in his throat. The best he could ever manage was, 'I should say something warm and round to you'. My producers and I would shake our heads in disbelief. But in truth, we never made any effort to praise him for trying to do his best. Because his praise was not in the form we wanted, we spurned it. At station meetings, he would indulge in platitudes or clichés which caused everyone to snort their derision.

Let me be clear. Praise or recognition is not flattery. Praise is not generalised 'strokes'. Praise is specific and personal. And above all, truthful and genuinely felt. Praise can take many forms and appear in many guises. In order to recognise it, you have to keep your eyes and ears open. Giving and receiving praise sounds so simple, but most of us are mean with genuine praise. Miserly even. And the meaner we are in giving it, the more we crave it for ourselves. Yet, much of how we behave or what we aim to achieve is consciously or unconsciously designed to gain praise. Mostly, if we are honest, we all secretly believe that we have never received the praise or recognition that we truly deserve.

Think again about occasions when your boss, your parent, your teacher, your lover, your child, your friend gave you genuine praise for something you had done. Write the occasions down. Add them to your list. Think about them. Have any of these occasions played a major part in who you are or the profession you chose?

When I was 14 and told to fill out a school form stating what I would do when I left school, I was at a total loss. My mother, having spent a great deal of her life in hospitals, wanted me to be a nurse. I knew, however, that I was not suited to this profession, because whenever another student threw up in class I would follow suit. So I would sit at my desk, chewing the end of my pen in genuine bewilderment. What would I do? I had no plan. No goals. None. Ruminating on this, I realise that mine was not an isolated case. As Gloria Steinem writes in her chapter in my book *Icons, Saints and Divas*, 'The ruling class plan for decades, even generations, the working class for Saturday night'. If you have something to preserve, something to pass on to the next generation, you teach them to plan their future. If you don't, then you accept what fate determines. Planning can be a form of praise, predicated as it is on a belief in that person's potential. My English teacher, Miss Elliott, observed me chewing the end of my pen and said, 'Susan, you have a problem?' When I said that I couldn't possibly fill out this form she snapped, 'Don't be ridiculous. Just put down that you will go to university'. When I protested, 'But no-one in my family has ever been to university', she said, 'There are teaching scholarships available and you will get one'.

'But what would I study?' I protested.

'English, of course.'

'Why?' I said.

'Because you can write.'

THINK AGAIN ABOUT OCCASIONS WHEN YOUR BOSS, YOUR PARENT, YOUR TEACHER, YOUR LOVER, YOUR CHILD, YOUR FRIEND GAVE YOU GENUINE PRAISE FOR SOMETHING YOU HAVE DONE. WRITE THE OCCASIONS DOWN.

In truth, no-one had ever told me this before. I had always gained good marks in English but I had never topped the class. Boldly, however, as instructed, I wrote down Bachelor of Arts. No big deal for some, but for me, at that stage of my life, it was something way beyond my expectations, a pipe dream. Later, however, it became a reality.

This was and is the power of good old-fashioned praise. It is freely available both to give and receive. There is no need for you to undertake rational emotive therapy or cognitive behavioural counselling or an in-depth analysis of your Oedipal traumas. Of course, if you have the time, the inclination and the money, go ahead. Most of us, however, do not.

Praise as the trigger, the catalyst, for boldness is the seed from which this book grew. I hope that my thoughts will help you rediscover the function of ordinary everyday praise in your life. Praise costs nothing. Takes practically no time. Praise is accessible to everyone. Even you.

Of course there is nothing new in this basic theory. In 1936 Dale Carnegie in the most popular self-help book in our time, *How to Win Friends and Influence People,* was probably the first to underline the dangers of criticism.

'When dealing with people, let us remember we are not dealing with creatures of logic. We are dealing with creatures of emotion, creatures bristling with prejudices and motivated by pride and vanity. And criticism is a dangerous spark — a spark that is liable to cause an explosion in the power magazine of pride.'

Many years ago when I first read this I dismissed it as Pollyanna polemic. Having now worked in the fields of education, communication and the media, I recognise it as the product of years of wisdom and experience in dealing with people.

If I am honest, and there's no point in not being honest in a book like this, I have been and probably still am on occasions much quicker to criticise than to praise. The clever crack, the tactless aside, the inability to resist the one-liner; my tongue has been a weapon against the barriers of class and gender. I know I have caused hurt and resentment that have rankled for years. Decades even.

To be fair, the importance of giving praise was not and is not part of the Western culture in which I was raised. Indeed, having a 'chop' at someone is a national sport in Australia. The British are less openly aggressive and are experts at damning with faint praise. The Americans often resort to flattery or cheap praise. Carnegie says, 'Flattery seldom works with discerning people. It is shallow, selfish and insecure. It ought to fail and it usually does'.

The problem is that so many people are so hungry for praise or recognition that they allow themselves to be deceived and therefore manipulated by flattery. Such people give praise a bad smell and cause us all to be suspicious and wary of those who give it genuinely.

I now believe, like Dale Carnegie, that we all crave praise, recognition and appreciation almost as much as we crave food. It would indeed be considered a crime if anyone let their family or their employees go without food for six days but as Carnegie says, 'They will let them go for six days, six weeks, sometimes sixty years without the kind words of appreciation that would sing in their memories for years'. Like everything else we learn, giving or withholding praise is a habit we learn early in life. Sometimes, even though we are given it, we don't recognise its power. It took me a long time to realise that the gift of my father's praise was the bedrock for everything that I ever achieved in my life. That, however, did not necessarily mean that I was as good at giving it as he was. It would take me some time to learn the habit of praise, even though I started my working life as an educator.

3

THE HABIT OF PRAISE

One of the most successful motivational books this decade is called *Awaken the Giant Within* by Anthony Robbins, a self-taught guru who not only writes books but gives advice to leading businessmen and politicians. He was a penniless janitor at twenty-four and a millionaire by thirty-four. The front cover of his book promises to teach you 'how to take immediate control of your mental, emotional, physical and financial destiny'. It was the word 'immediate' that concerned me. I suppose that you could make an immediate change to your consciousness by reading a book that gave you a sense of your own potential. And the first step towards any change is to actually seed it in the mind. And, after all, those thousands of people who attend his seminars and testify to the amazing results they have had in improving the quality of their lives can't all be wrong or deluded.

There are days in my life when I would be perfectly happy just to 'awaken the pygmy' within myself, let alone unleash the giant. Appetite for food and pleasure seems to be the only giant that I have ever been able to awaken in myself.

I have researched scores of this style of book and interviewed many of their authors and one theme that they all have in common is the need for us all to build and maintain our confidence, our self-esteem. We have to learn to believe in ourselves and our ability to reach our goals. No-one would disagree with this as a premise. The point is how do we achieve this?

Believing in yourself is a form of self-praise but I do not think you can believe in yourself immediately, simply by deciding to. Given that we all possess the ability to praise ourselves and others, the question becomes how do we acquire the habit? Like all habits, it takes time, and practice. Day after day of being conscious of what you are thinking and saying and doing.

At one stage of writing this book I was in the country at a friend's farm. As we both were locked into the discipline of writing every day we decided to put ourselves on a health-kick regime. You know the theory — clear the body of toxins and you clear the mind. Day One was fruit. Any fruit, any amount, but nothing but fruit. And lots of water. No alcohol. No coffee. 'After all,' I said to myself, 'this is what all the self-help books teach'. Life is like a healthy diet. You have to take each day at a time, keep your goals clear, concentrate on the positive, eliminate the negative, have a role model, don't associate with negative people, maintain your momentum and if you fail then just learn from it and keep going. All sounds so simple, doesn't it? All you have to change are your bad habits. Sure. After three days of no cheating when my friend had lost three pounds and I had lost nothing I gave up. My body had given me no recognition of discipline and denial.

If you have ever tried to give up smoking you know exactly how hard it is. But millions and millions of people have done it. You start by making a decision and acting on it. Whatever the complex and varied reasons people give for quitting smoking, the truth is they did it because they knew it was a killer and they wanted to live. Giving up something that is destructive is a form of praise to yourself. I really loved to smoke. Now, like so many others, I can't stand the smell of a cigarette and would never be tempted to try one even for old time's sake. I simply, day by day, lost the habit of smoking. The problem with eating of course is that we have to do it to survive. It's what we eat and how much that can kill us. Anthony Robbins was also fat as well as poor before he wrote his first book. Now that gives me hope.

Most of us when confronted with how and when we give or receive praise are not always accurate in our assessment. I always thought that I was warm, grateful and gracious when someone praised me. It wasn't until I was with a friend walking down the street and a stranger stopped to compliment me on my television program that after he had walked on, my friend said, 'You were really quite rude to that person'. I said, 'Nonsense. I wasn't. I smiled and thanked him'. 'Oh sure,' she said, 'but you looked down at your feet, shuffled and didn't continue the conversation'. And I had to admit it was true. My intention was not to be rude but I was insensitive to the courage and the boldness of the person who had stopped me in the street to praise me.

HOW OFTEN HAVE WE DEALT WITH EVEN A SMALL COMPLIMENT LIKE, 'I LOVE YOUR BLOUSE OR YOUR DRESS' WITH 'WHAT, THIS OLD THING. I'VE HAD IT FOR YEARS', OR 'REALLY? I'VE NEVER LIKED IT MUCH'.

When I analysed my reaction to being praised I realised that when it was unexpected I did not know how to deal with it. I was embarrassed, not in control and not wanting to appear to be over-impressed by what the person was saying.

How often have we dealt with even a small compliment like, 'I love your blouse or your dress' with, 'What, this old thing. I've had it for years', or 'Really? I've never liked it much'.

And yet secretly we are quite chuffed. 'Well, fancy them saying that.' Or else suspicious. 'What did they want from me?'

What we have really done by those reactions is throw praise back in that person's face. You can bet it's the last time they'll say that to you, or anybody else, for awhile.

This is a habit that you can easily change. Normally, if you are embarrassed by receiving praise you are also reluctant to give it. So, now, wherever you are reading this, say something to someone, even a stranger, which praises or compliments them. Go on, do it.

Now. I don't care if you are on the bus or in a coffee shop. If you are alone, pick up the phone. Just do it.

Like any habit, you have to repeat it as often as possible before it becomes almost automatic. Remember when you first learnt to drive a car and you thought that you would never be able to keep your eye on the rear-vision mirror, change gears, flick the indicators and turn the wheel at the same time. After doing it often enough, you don't even think about it.

If you treat the habit of praise like learning a new skill, you can re-invent the way you treat yourself and other people. However, like any skill, you have to continue to practise in order to be really good. You would accept this if, for example, you wished to be a good tennis player or a pianist. You would know that such pursuits involve hours and hours of repetitive practice. If someone throws your attempts at praise back in your face, then don't give up. Try again. And again. No-one can resist goodwill forever.

And if you fail or mess up in your attempts, then don't criticise yourself. Criticism works no more effectively with adults than it does with children. And at heart we are all children. I would always chant the mantra to my creative writing classes, 'There is no such thing as failure, only feedback'. You must use your experience to keep going, not to stop. Sometimes you cannot believe how hard it is to praise either yourself or other people. Many people prefer to have a pessimistic view of life because it's more predictable. Pessimism is a self-fulfilling prophecy. But optimism can be learned.

One of the suggestions in most of the motivational books is to find a role model to help and guide you. Even better, a mentor.

People come up to me after concerts, and tell me I'm a role model. It's not just from women either. At one concert I received some really nice fanmail from a fisherman on the Western Australian coast, who said, 'I came all the way to see the concert, and it was really fantastic. You really gave me confidence in my energy, and it really stirred things up that had

*been dormant for a while, and thanks. And if you
ever want to come out to the coast, there's this
place.' That's fantastic. It means it's a kind of
disassociated energy that I can give people.*

ROBYN ARCHER *Tall Poppies Too*

*I did the promotion in the middle of a
heartbreaking end to a four-year relationship. I
came back to this country feeling completely
shocked at my experience in Britain. I talked to my
grandmother. At eighty-two, she was able to put
things in perspective and say things like, 'Big
advances have always been heralded by sniping
and attacks.' What also made it easier were the
letters that started coming in. That's always been
my publishing experience, that controversy will be
raging in the newspapers or among the cultural
elite and in the meantime I'm getting all these
letters from women saying this is absolutely right.
In the end that is the real thing, that's the only
thing that counts.*

NAOMI WOLF *Icons, Saints and Divas*

When I was young I knew that I was not fulfilling my potential but
I was uncertain of how to go about it. I didn't know anyone whom
I considered really successful and there were no books that told the
true stories, warts and all, of the lives of successful women.

All my life it seemed I had been searching for heroines, for
something or someone positive to believe in, to base my life on.
Georgie in the *Famous Five* books was, for many of us, one of the
few confident, assertive female role models we ever had. The other
one I identified with was Jo from *Little Women*, who was of course
a fictionalised version of Louisa May Alcott herself. I know the
book well. I was given it five years in a row from under the
Christmas tree at my father's work party.

Much later when reading Deirdre Bair's award-winning biography of Simone de Beauvoir, I learnt that the young Simone also identified heavily with the character of Jo. She said that reading *Little Women* gave her an exalted sense of herself and she felt such esteem for Jo that she could tell herself that it didn't matter if society was cruel or unjust because, like Jo, she too could make choices and achieve a place for herself in society. C. S. Lewis was right when he said we read in order to feel less alone.

> *What I always hear from readers is, 'You validated me and you made me know I'm not alone, I'm not a freak, I'm not the only one who has felt that way'. Yesterday I was at an Israeli Expo conference and all these Israeli women who had read my first book came up to me and said, 'You liberated me. After I read your book I went out and slept with this one, this one, and this one'. They read it in Hebrew twenty-two years ago, so there was a sense that women often feel very dirty about themselves and self-abnegating, as if they're the only ones who ever did this. It was a book that made you feel good about yourself and your sexuality and made you feel less lonely.*
> *That was not my intent. But books do reach out beyond the skin and make people feel joined in some way. There is a sense in which you should be changed by reading a book.*
> ERICA JONG *Icons, Saints and Divas*

As my area of study had been literature, I decided to write my first book based on interviews with Australian women writers, secretly of course hoping to discover how one became bold enough to become a writer. Where do you start? I applied for a small research grant with an academic colleague but just when we were awarded the money she decided she was not interested in pursuing it and I was at a loss.

I know now that without the encouragement and praise of a close friend who not only said, 'Of course you can do it on your own' but suggested that I expand the book to include the life stories of women who had succeeded in a wide range of professions, I would never have begun. She not only encouraged me by recommending a few of her friends and colleagues but offered to come along to the first interviews with me. Her belief in my ability was the catalyst for me, not only to not give up but to be bold enough to go outside my area of knowledge and expand my horizons. I researched, I talked to many people and finally made a short list. All the women had to have struggled and worked hard to achieve success. I didn't consider anyone who was born to it, married into it or landed it by luck. I chose a broad range of ethnic, educational, professional and class backgrounds but most importantly those chosen had to tell me the true story of their lives and their struggle to succeed.

With a tentative hand I dialled their numbers, introduced myself, told them about my project and to my amazement, without exception, they agreed. What I hadn't realised then was that even the act of asking people to tell you the story of their lives is a form of praise. Most people are never asked to answer questions for the purpose of publication in a newspaper, magazine or book but the act of asking someone about themselves, purely out of interest and actively listening to their answers is a form of praise.

When I came away from those first few interviews, I felt so positive and powerful that I knew these women's life stories would make other people feel powerful too. They give you the feeling of, 'If she's done it, so can I' and I still get letters from women and men telling me how these stories changed their lives and gave them the confidence to do something they've always wanted to do. Not only was there a crying need for a book about successful Australian women, but also for a book that was positive — a book that encouraged you to grow, that said, 'Get out there and be a success — fulfil your potential'.

These interviews, begun so tentatively, became the basis for my first book *Tall Poppies*. Now if I tell you that it was an overnight best-seller, will you think that I am boasting or blowing my own trumpet? This is the dilemma with which we are all faced when talking of our own successes, isn't it? The messages we are given are so contradictory.

On the one hand, my Mother's favourite
'Self praise is no recommendation',
and on the other
'There's no point in hiding your light under a bushel'.
On the one hand
'Be self-effacing, don't sing your own praises',
on the other
'If you don't believe in yourself no-one else will'.
And yet the stories we want so much, the stories we pay to hear, are those told by successful people about themselves.

General Norman Schwarzkopf reputedly earned between $130,000 and $190,000 for an hour's presentation at the Sydney Entertainment Centre. He was joined by three other high-profile people who also talked about themselves and their own experiences. The crowd was estimated to be 7000 people. I don't think many people would have turned up to listen to a self-confessed failure or even to someone who was so self-effacing that they constantly down-played their achievements, do you?

Even to appear in a book titled *Tall Poppies* made those women objects of envy and derision. I was guilty just by association.

Not that the women in the book were daunted by other people's envy. It is, they all knew, an unfortunate by-product of success. People only envy what secretly they most admire, which is why envy is one of the most destructive emotions. It takes courage to admit your envy, to come face to face with it, and to deal with it. The 'tall poppy' syndrome, so prevalent in Australian and British culture, is really just a fancy name for plain, unadorned envy. It is based, however, on a misunderstanding of how success really works. Those people who expend their energies trying to cut successful people down, imagine success is like a pie. And if someone gets a slice of it, then there is less for everyone else. Success is, however, more like a magic pudding; the more you take from it, the bigger it grows. Every time someone succeeds in a new area, their success opens it up for others to follow.

Professor Norman Feather of Flinders University has undertaken research in the 'tall poppy syndrome' particularly in relation to students in high school, where habits are not just learned but cemented, often for life.

The term 'tall poppy', he informs us, has a long history; its origins go back to ancient times. 'The Roman historian Livy refers to the symbolic decapitation of the heads of the tallest poppies by the elder Tarquinius when the Roman ruler was walking in the garden. This message was conveyed to his son, Sextus Tarquinius, who then rid himself of the chief men of the state of Gabii and thus delivered the state, unresisting, to the Roman king'.

The message of 'destroy the leaders' if you want to attain power, has of course continued throughout history. Professor Feather's research, however, was more concerned with tall poppies who are viewed impersonally from a distance, rather than those who are competitive rivals in a struggle for power. We view such people as presidents or prime ministers, kings or queens, high-profile entertainers, business leaders and high-status people in other areas like the arts from a distance. We do not know them personally but we know them through the mass media and therefore feel free to have opinions on their fall from status or power.

Although the results from Professor Feather's research are more complex than are relevant to this discussion, some salient points can be made. He found that a person's attitude towards tall poppies related to that person's level of self-esteem and competence. Those students with low self-esteem and low perceived personal competence were more likely to favour the fall of tall poppies.

Interestingly, when Australia is compared with Japan, where the cultural saying is, 'the nail that sticks up must be nailed down', the Japanese emphasis on modesty and self-effacement discourages individuals that stand out from the group norm; the Japanese emphasis is on enforcing conformity, the Australian emphasis is egalitarianism. Both cultures, however, discourage the tall poppy from flourishing.

For the purposes of my argument, it therefore follows that the more students, teachers and parents are encouraged in the habit of praise, the more their self-esteem will be raised and the less malicious they will be when a high achiever suffers a fall in status.

It is of course important to distinguish between good and bad tall poppies. 'Bad' tall poppies who are proven to be corporate liars and cheats deserve to be brought to justice, but people who are attacked simply because they are perceived to have achieved too much public success only satiate the public's appetite for destructive criticism.

It needs to be pointed out to people who constantly indulge in tall-poppy lopping that all it reflects is their own envy and low self-esteem and that they and the community would be much better served if they got on with building up their own self-esteem and fulfilled some of their own secretly held goals. A culture that constantly urges everyone to be individually responsible for their own success and well-being and then condones the cutting down of those who stand out from the crowd will never reach its full potential. It is not enough to say that you support success, you must act to prove that you mean it. An entire culture must learn the habit of praise, attack the habit of envy and reward those who succeed — the good poppies.

One of the women in *Tall Poppies*, the late Elizabeth Riddell, a highly respected doyenne of Australian journalism, freely admitted that all her decisions in life were based on instinct. Her belief in herself was there from the beginning, almost innate. She said, 'I never had any doubt that I could do anything'. When she received her first job offer, which meant she had to leave her home in New Zealand and go to Australia to work on a newspaper, she said her mother did the greatest thing that mothers can do for their children, 'She let me go'. To trust in your child's ability to deal with life's setbacks and opportunities is the highest form of praise you can give.

Although intellectually Riddell said she was a pessimist, in practice she was optimistic. When she woke up in the morning she thought, 'today's going to be all right'. Life's transience, 'the fact that nothing lasts', was what she believed makes everything so good. That's why she had a life, into her nineties, so rich and so full of experience.

And yet when I was at a publicity lunch at the Sydney Hilton, it was Betty Riddell who said in front of 400 people, 'All this talk about "best" and "top" and "success" worries me. Is it really necessary to talk about it?'

'I USED TO TURN MYSELF INSIDE OUT TO BE ONE OF THE GOOD STUDENTS, BUT I NEVER GOT THE FLOWERS. IT WASN'T UNTIL YEARS LATER THAT I REALISED THAT THE REASON I DIDN'T GET THEM WAS BECAUSE I WAS THE OUTSIDER.'

Pat O'Shane, now a magistrate, another guest on the panel at the Sydney Hilton, said she loved to talk about success and achievement, and to receive praise, as all her life she had been struggling against being treated as lesser because she was Aboriginal and a woman. She told a story about how when she was in primary school at the end of the week the teacher would give the classroom flowers to the best student. 'I used to turn myself inside out to be one of the good students, but I never got the flowers. It wasn't until years later that I realised that the reason I didn't get them was because I was the outsider.'

Rather than dwell on the hurt that she felt, she used it as a spur to achieve higher and higher things. And it worked. Her Aboriginal mother imbued in her that she was as good as anybody else and her Irish father taught her to fight for the causes she believed in. Despite a major breakdown and having to fight the doctor's recommendation for a lobotomy operation, she graduated in law and became a well-known spokesperson for Aboriginal rights.

For O'Shane the greatest praise is when Aboriginal women, whom she has never met, come up to her in the street, put their arms around her and tell her what she has done for them.

'That really makes me feel good. I feel as if I am home when they tell me that.'

The third panel member, Maggie Tabberer, the style queen of the Australian fashion industry, has received a great deal of praise throughout her life for her beauty, her style and her many achievements. And yet she began her career as a single mother with two little girls to support and no financial backing or formal education. She realised very early that there is no point in just thinking positively about your career, you have to actively do something. You have to take the plunge. She freely admitted that she overcommitted herself in order not to think about the enormity of what she tackled. It is through working hard that she has gained a strong sense of herself. It gave her a bedrock of experience.

> *I'm a fairly optimistic person ... If everything that*
> *I'm involved in now suddenly fell away, I know I*
> *would cope because I've coped before.*

The women in *Tall Poppies* succeeded in whatever they chose to pursue because whether innately or by the use of role models or by circumstances catapulting them into vulnerable situations they had to believe in themselves. They all knew that whatever confronted them, they would be able to deal with it. Many times in their lives it wasn't easy, but the ingrained habit of believing in themselves, however they acquired it, played a major part in their success.

As I first wrote in the introduction to *Tall Poppies*, 'Where does that will to succeed, that relentless persistence to explore your full potential come from? These women's stories suggest that it is based in having a strong belief in yourself, in your own worth, a confidence in using the pronoun "I"'. Now as I write this book, many years later, I realise that the answer lies in praise. As the people responsible for guiding the child into adulthood, parents and the way they use praise are crucial to how we view ourselves.

The old Jesuit saying about 'give me a child for the first seven years and he is mine forever' has now been refined by scientists to the first three years. They believe that what we absorb, how we are treated, in our first three years, will be very influential in determining most of our behaviour for the rest of our lives. If you are unfortunate enough not to have been praised in your formative years, then the sooner you realise this and attempt to counteract its effects, the better.

4

PARENTS: THINKING PRAISE

* Patterns
* Language
* Trust
* Responsibility
* Struggle

As I was writing the early drafts of this chapter, the Australian Open Tennis Championships were on and during my recreation breaks, when I was watching the tennis players sweating and battling it out against one another, I began to realise that in spite of their fitness, their training programs, their skills, their talent, that each match was won or lost in the players' minds between the end of one point and the beginning of another.

What they were thinking about themselves and their performance ultimately made the difference between winning and losing. What happens in our heads is the engine that drives us, whether on the tennis court or in any other aspect of life. Anyone who has ever played sport knows this. Thinking that you are going to miss the point or the goal and you most surely will. Thinking that you will win will not automatically make it happen but it will make it much more likely.

So why do we practise in sport what we fail to practise in our everyday lives? Many of the tennis players who were playing in the Australian Open had their proud parents sitting in the stands. But even if, for whatever reason, they weren't there, most sportspeople who get to the top ranks have parents who have backed them all the way in order that they explore their talent to the full.

Pat Rafter, the Australian who won the 1997 US Open Tennis Singles did not come from a financially privileged background but his parents told the world that they always believed in him and always believed he would make it to the top. That belief seeds itself into the mind of the young child.

Whatever it is that a child is attempting, to have a parent say, 'I believe in you' is the catalyst for the child to begin to believe in him or herself. This is the beginning of taking risks, the beginning of boldness.

Time and again, the tennis commentators pointed out that if players mishit a shot or had luck go against them, how they reacted to this was all important. Coaches who are paid to have total belief in their players and spend a great deal of time trying to get inside the players' heads in order to train them to think positively and not overreact to mistakes, are always using psychological techniques in order to achieve the maximum results.

What used to be called day-dreaming is now termed visualisation and all sports players are trained prior to the match to visualise themselves playing the game and winning it. Thinking praise is called giving yourself affirmations. These are considered essential when the match isn't going well. Regardless of how you view this new-age jargon, it was practised long before self-help gurus took it up.

Harry Hopman, one of the great tennis coaches, always emphasised to his players that when you are down is no time to lose faith and start playing it safe. This, he said, is exactly the time when you must keep going for your shots, even harder.

Going for your best shots is of course easier to do when you are playing well. Unlike life, when you hit a great shot in tennis there is instant applause. In opera, when you hit a top note, there is instant cheering and 'bravos'. When you fail to do your best, however, there is silence and in that silence what you think in your own head will decide whether you persist and, with determination, win through.

Whenever Pete Sampras got a bad call or had bad luck, you would see the steely determination fix in his face. After this, was when he would serve an ace.

John McEnroe, who was in the commentators' box and now plays Seniors' tennis, however, had a different technique. When he was a player, he would abuse the umpire, create a disturbance, swear, storm around the court, jeer at the crowd; almost as if he had to get rid of all the pent up, negative emotion before he could focus and recover his power. This tactic worked for him and probably unnerved his opponents, but most players go downhill once they start to lose control. McEnroe, however, never really lost control.

Tennis demonstrates that there is no one way to control what the voice inside your head is saying to you, but you must find a way whereby that voice continues to believe in you, continues to praise you. Early patterns of behaviour are very hard to break, but tennis players are proof that they can be broken. We continually see players, who seem unable to get on top again once they are behind in the score, suddenly find a way of breaking their old destructive patterns and winning through. There is always a way, but it has to begin in the mind. Parents and teachers are really like sports coaches in that the early patterns they encourage in children are imprinted in their minds.

Parents of course have, or should have, a life-long commitment to believing in their children and thus transferring that pattern of belief to the child. What the parent says to the child about him or herself will imprint itself on the child and become part of the child's inner voice. The salient difference is that parents coach for life and coaches coach for the match or the season. You never hear a good coach tell any of his or her players that they are stupid or useless or hopeless. Nor do you ever hear a good parent use those words about their children. Bad parents use them all the time but they are probably the same words that they heard as children. And so patterns, good and bad, are repeated. Dietitians may tell us that we are what we eat, but I think what comes out of our mouths in terms of the words we use are much more self-defining. The old adage that we don't use language, language uses us, is very relevant.

Merely changing your use of language can be very liberating. For example, people inevitably ask children, 'What is your name?' When the ideas for this book were still percolating, a couple of my close friends had a daughter later in life than planned. When we were all sitting around the table discussing the best way to coach a little girl into becoming a confident woman, I conducted my first experiment.

As soon as she could say her name, I taught her to say whenever she was asked her name, 'I'm Georgia. And I'm fantastic'. I observed the smiling reactions from her questioners, which in turn caused her to smile. She only ever received positive feedback. She is now six and a confident, articulate little girl who leaps at every invitation to visit someone new, go to a camp, write a poem, paint a sketch. Her parents have consciously pursued the 'only praise' rule.

My theory was reinforced when I read that Donald McDonald, Chair of the ABC, was asked how his family life contributed to his success and he said, 'I came from a sociable sort of family. The dictum was you praise and you praise greatly — a sort of generosity of support. I can't remember ever being criticised as a child. I can't remember being punished ever'.

Wendy Sharpe, the artist, won the prestigious Archibald Prize at the age of 36. Her winning self-portrait satirised the concept of the artist as a hero. She is described as portraying herself 'in acid-green bra, leopard-print pants and rubber thongs hamming it up as Diana, goddess of the hunt, in all her rude glory'. She has never been shy about placing herself in her work, nude or clothed or wearing silly hats. Now that is bold.

Nor is she daunted by rejection. In fact, when rejected, she immediately tries again. 'The first year the Möet et Chandon (art prize) was run, I put something in and got rejected. That same day I took the same painting across to the Art Gallery of New South Wales and won the Sulman Prize.' To be rejected and immediately try again is based on a strong sense of self-worth.

So where does that self-belief and resilience come from? She said her parents praised her, a lot, and encouraged her artistic gifts. She admitted that she soaked up praise like her canvasses soaked up paint. 'When I was a child it was fun to show off my paintings to everybody. It was good attention'.

But of course there are always children who don't seem to be able to respond to straightforward praise, and with whom, with the best will in the world, parents find themselves in conflict. In these cases, praise needs to take another form. After the argument or fight, explain to the child what you want him or her to do. And then say, 'I'm going to leave it with you'. Then with your hand on their shoulder add, 'But I believe you can do it'. If you see them struggling with it, say, 'I know you're struggling and I'm proud of you'. Rather than relying on punishment, put the responsibility for the problem back on the child and then tell them that you believe in their ability to solve it. Remember that whatever words you use to describe your children will stick in their minds for a very long time, as do rewards and punishments.

RATHER THAN RELYING ON PUNISHMENT, PUT THE RESPONSIBILITY FOR THE PROBLEM BACK ON THE CHILD AND THEN TELL THEM THAT YOU BELIEVE IN THEIR ABILITY TO SOLVE IT. REMEMBER THAT WHATEVER WORDS YOU USE TO DESCRIBE YOUR CHILDREN WILL STICK IN THEIR MINDS FOR A VERY LONG TIME, AS DO REWARDS AND PUNISHMENTS.

When I was in year seven, my best friend came top of the class. 'Come on', I said, 'let's go and see my Mum. She'll be so pleased'. My mother praised her generously and gave her five dollars. Thrilled, we skipped off to her house. When she showed her mother what my mother had given her, her mother replied, 'I suppose that means I've got to match it, does it?' and took the money very begrudgingly out of her purse. The mother's lack of praise and generosity meant there was no real joy for my friend in those treats she bought for us with the money. Neither of us ever spoke about her mother's response. Three years later, when we were putting rollers in our hair in preparation for the school dance, we heard her mother telling a neighbour over the back fence, 'She may be good at school but she's so plain, she'll never get a husband'. Sometimes parents, particularly mothers who have not had the opportunities that their daughters enjoy, are envious of them. The 'tall poppy' syndrome can exist within a family.

My best friend was the only one in our university group not to finish her degree because she married the first man who asked her.

> *I don't think anyone ever took away from me who I*
> *basically was at my centre. My parents communicated*
> *to me — how ever they did it I don't even know, and*
> *I don't think they even know — a tremendous sense*
> *of freedom. And they also communicated to me that*
> *it was okay to be an artist. How they did that I'm*
> *not sure because in some ways they didn't even give*
> *themselves permission to be that.*
>
> ERICA JONG *Icons, Saints and Divas*

> *My mother thought I was a genius. She said I drew a*
> *perfect banana when I was less than two years old*
> *and I never talked until I was a year old but then,*
> *when I did, I used full sentences. I don't know that*
> *in my household that meant a great deal. My mother*
> *had no education herself but she revered it. She was a*
> *woman of great sensitivity more than commonsense.*
> *She was a thoughtful person and she had examined*
> *the way other people raised children. Most women of*
> *her generation did not think about it, they just did it.*

And if they'd been yelled at and spanked and beaten
that's what they did to their kids.
All the kids on my block were treated that way. Not
us. She had great ambition for me. She went to
work when I was quite young to save money so I
could go to college. As it turned out she couldn't
help me in the end, when I did go, but she tried. She
wanted to, she foresaw, but she didn't ever push me.
In some households if a mother thought a child was
bright and didn't have much ambition for herself, if
she planted her hopes in the child, which my mother
did in me, she would have pushed that child or put
pressure on her in some way, but my mother never
did that.

MARILYN FRENCH *Icons, Saints and Divas*

Tell a child they're clever

they're good looking,
they're good fun.

Come to think of it,
Tell an adult they're clever
they're good looking,
they're good fun.

But first you must start with yourself. What is your standard reply whenever someone asks the standard question, 'How are you?' Do you say, 'I'm OK' or
  'Not bad'
  or 'I'm great'
  or 'I'm fantastic'
  or 'I'm brilliant'?
Try to work out why you always reply in the same way. Whatever your usual reply, try taking it up the scale a few notches. Experiment using superlatives. Use words you have never used

before in your life. And if you are asked why, then make up something praiseworthy about yourself — the first thing that comes to mind.

Practise this consistently for a week. Write down what words you used, what the other person's reaction was and how using this language made you feel.

Once you have started to change your own language patterns regarding yourself, start to use them on other people like your children, your parents, your work colleagues. If they start to suspect that you are either going mad, having an affair or sending them up, explain what you are doing. Confess that you think you have been rather mean with the language you have used and that you are attempting to be more generous. If they are still suspicious then blame me, blame this book. If you start to think praise and speak praise both about yourself and others, even if it begins as a game, once the pattern is set then boldness will not be far away.

SHE SAID THEY WERE SO TERRIFIED OF USING SUPERLATIVES THAT WHEN THE AMERICAN TELEVISION SERIES CALLED *IT'S INCREDIBLE* CAME TO NEW ZEALAND THEY RENAMED IT *THAT'S FAIRLY INTERESTING.*

Above all, if you are going to praise someone, be generous. So often we hold back. The most some people seem capable of saying after any experience, however enjoyable, is 'quite nice'. Or if someone does something really well, they say 'you were quite good'. BAN THE WORD 'QUITE'. BE GENEROUS OR SHUT UP. Sometimes the reluctance to use superlatives is cultural.

Jane Campion, director of the internationally acclaimed film *The Piano,* believes that because her home country, New Zealand, was a utopian settlement based on ideas of equality, nobody was encouraged or indeed allowed to excel. It was a culture that was very uncelebratory. She said they were so terrified of using superlatives that when the American television series called *It's Incredible* came to New Zealand they renamed it *That's Fairly Interesting.*

What are the reasons for our reluctance to praise generously? One of the factors that reinforces our shyness, our reluctance to break out of our old habits, is the fear that people will laugh at us. It always seems safer to stay with the small, inconspicuous, predictable words and not draw attention to oneself. We miss out on so many opportunities in life because we allow our shyness, our insecurity about ourselves, to take control. Sometimes it's just downright meanness. You won't give someone the praise you crave for yourself. The only way to overcome this is to act. Starting with the words you use is a first step.

When someone asks you to describe your life, do you tell it as a tragic tale or a drama or a comedy or a boring list of non-events? So often the way people view themselves, and what the voice inside their head tells them, is dictated by the words they use to describe their past life. Robyn Nevin, a highly successful actor and theatre director, remembers vividly the tragic aura with which she used to surround herself and the incident that was the catalyst for changing the way she viewed herself.

> *At one stage I lived with a very famous Sydney identity who ran a boarding house. I was just out of acting school and must have been feeling very sorry for myself. I was telling her my tragic story and she thought it was the funniest thing she ever heard. She laughed so much she literally wet her pants. I got a terrific fright. It was really good for me. That was the beginning of my learning that you can't go on hanging onto your tragic past.*
>
> *Tall Poppies*

So often when I speak at conferences, lunches or dinners, people come up to me and start to tell me the sad story of their lives. Sometimes when I look hard at them I imagine that I can see dozens of bulging garbage bags attached to very long strings behind them. No wonder they can't move forward with all this rotten garbage weighing them down with every step. The garbage of the past has to be dealt with, you can't keep dragging it around with you. If you can't dump it in the bin where it belongs, then seek professional help from someone who can help you do it. The first step is to listen to the words that you use to describe your past. If you change the words, you change your attitude. There is a very fine line between tragedy and comedy — usually just a few key words. When I was a child there was a saying 'sticks and stones can break my bones but names can never hurt me'.

They can of course. But only if you let them.

SUMMARY
1. Think of yourself not so much as a parent but as a sports coach.
2. As a parent/coach you have to convey total belief in your player.
   'I believe in you' is one of the most powerful things a parent can say to a child.
3. Teach your child to only think praise. Teach them to dispel any negative thoughts.
4. When things go wrong, train your child to react positively and not overreact to mistakes.
5. Change the language you use with your child. When praising, praise lavishly, using only superlatives.
6. Encourage your child to believe in themselves by the language they use.
7. Encourage children to respond to rejection by being bold, or bolder — try a bigger and better opportunity.
8. Start with the language you use about yourself — upgrade your daily response to the ubiquitous, 'How are you?'
9. Let go of the things in your past that are weighing you down. Dump them in the bin.
10. Tell someone the tragic events in your life as if they are comic.

5

EDUCATION: ONLY PRAISE

* Goals
* Problem solving
* Success/Failure
* Rewards/Punishment
* Persistence

I spent over 20 years of my life teaching students, firstly at high school level and then mostly at university. I consider it to have been a privilege. However, unlike infant and primary students, by the time students reached university level, many of their patterns of behaviour had been set. The earlier the habit of praise is used and practised daily in education, the better, because it enables everyone to expand their knowledge and stretch their horizons. I firmly believe that you cannot praise a child too much or encourage them too much. This does not mean that you do not balance this with honest feedback, but it should always be framed in a positive way. There will be enough people attempting to criticise or pull them down later in their lives.

All formal education begins with reading. Children who are lucky enough to have someone read them a story when they are fresh from the bath and snuggled up in bed will all their lives associate reading with pleasure. To have a parent's total attention at the end of the day, no matter what, is indeed a form of praise, a recognition that the child is important and that reading is important. Whenever a child reads to you, give them praise. Such children will be eager to read for themselves and to give that pleasure to others by reading to them. I was one of these children and taught myself to read before I went to school. On my first day at school, I stood up and proudly read everything the teacher had written on the blackboard, expecting the kind of praise I received from parents and relations when I read from a book or a newspaper at home. Instead, stunned and wide-eyed with shock, the teacher's words of reprimand stung my cheeks as if she had slapped them. I was told not to stand up, not to talk out of turn and to read only at the same pace as everyone else in the class. I spent the next hour standing in the back of the classroom with my hands over my eyes. Hopefully that style of teacher has long gone from the system. Punishment of that sort for a child not fortified, like me, by praise from home could be destructive for the rest of that child's life. For various reasons, trauma associated with reading still affects many children. And literacy can be a major problem, particularly for adults, whose entire lives have been ruined because they never learnt the basic skills of reading and never associated it with pleasure, only with terror.

Sometimes a lateral approach works best. One of my friend's children was having great difficulty learning to read, and despite everyone's best efforts, he had simply refused to talk about it or even pick up a book. He was also having difficulty learning to ride a bike. One day I simply said, 'Come on, let's go for a ride'. He said, 'I can't'. I said, 'You can't now, but by the end of the day you will — it doesn't matter if you fall off — let's go to the oval where it's soft'. Thus I conveyed to him my total confidence that he could learn to ride while at the same time letting him know that if he fell off a few times, it didn't matter. Freeing him from the fear of failure and giving him the confidence to succeed was all it took. The very next day he picked up a book and began to read. He also learnt to ride a bike that day, but not without a few skinned knees.

In all learning, 'readiness' as the educational philosopher Piaget said, 'is everything'. When you are ready to absorb the information or the skills, as long as someone doesn't criticise your early efforts, you will succeed. It's good to have goals as long as they don't become inhibiting reminders of what you have failed to achieve by a certain time. Goals often imply a direct lineal path from desire to attainment. Very often, however, the indirect route is the one that leads to success, particularly if the well-trodden path has previously led to failure.

When I was teaching in an impoverished south London school, where most of the students were West Indian whose grasp of the English language was tenuous, I found that what they most liked to do was play act. By allowing them to enact various scenes from soap operas or their own domestic lives, they lost their self-consciousness. I used these dramatisations as a starting point for them to write down what they had just experienced. And then, working from their own writing, I was able to give them the confidence to progress with their use of language.

Similarly, with a class of teenagers in Australia, most of whom had already failed their major English exam twice, I set up a situation whereby they tried to put the language of Shakespeare into their own words. Even the name Shakespeare daunted them, let alone the use of Elizabethan language. Mind you, changing, 'You inviolable wretch' to 'You fat turd', did nothing for the language but it certainly demystified a text that they had all previously refused to read. Having done this, they no longer felt that literature was something outside their reach. I think Shakespeare would have approved of my motives if not my methods.

So much of what we achieve at school depends on the expectations of the teachers. If you know that the teacher believes in you and expects you to do well, then you are more than halfway towards fulfilling those expectations. There is a well-documented experiment where the teachers of two classes were told that one class was extremely bright and the other not so bright. The results of the experiment proved that each class achieved according to the expectations of their teachers. The so-called 'bright' students did much better than the others. The truth was that the classes consisted of roughly the same mixed abilities.

In some educational circles today, competition, if not a dirty word, is a source of controversy. One of the unfortunate by-products of our attempts to give all students an equal chance to pursue their talents and thus fulfil their potential, is that by downplaying competition, we have down-graded success, whereas everyone should be given a chance to succeed at something and receive praise for it. I once taught a secondary student who could hardly read a line but who did wonderful imitations of a dog barking. While working on his reading skills, I found a play which required barking dogs and he had his moment of glory. If a child is having difficulty learning a task, then find something else for which you can give them praise.

By refusing to grade students' work or allowing someone to win a competition, you rob the student of the satisfaction that comes from knowing she or he did something really well. The real point of education should be to allow enough diversity in the curriculum and the student activities to enable most students to succeed at something and thus be praised for doing so. Without real competition, you breed mediocrity.

The truly damaging aspect of competition is when teachers grade a student as a zero. One of my friends, who is now a highly successful bureaucrat, had her creativity totally stifled at an early age by receiving a zero for an original story. The topic she was given was 'A night prowler' and she wrote a story about a snail eating the delphiniums at night in the garden. Rather than the teacher explaining that she had misunderstood what was intended by the topic, the teacher gave her a feeling of shame and worthlessness in terms of her ability to write, which stayed with her for the rest of her life. Nothing that anyone says or does should ever place limitations upon a person's creativity. All creative or lateral thinking should be praised — highly praised.

Criticism, whether open or masked by laughter, is always damaging because it blocks off the chance of the person ever risking that activity in the same way again. There are ways of giving negative feedback that are not damaging.

It took me twenty years before I confessed to my parents why, at the age of five, I returned home early from my first gym class in my new gym clothes and shoes, and announced that I did not like it and wouldn't be returning. No amount of questioning, prying or cajoling on the part of my parents could get me to give any explanation. The truth was that the teacher had asked all the girls to do a cartwheel across the room. This was a skill that I had tried to master many times on the front lawn, my only witness being my dog Chips. That first gym lesson I failed again to complete the wheel. And every time I tried, my efforts became more hopeless. By the time I had reached the other side of the hall, not only was the class laughing but the teacher was leading them. Standing there in my little black gym shorts I truly wanted to die.

These incidents appear petty when you retell them as adults, but I know that everyone who is honest has similar anecdotes, which, although decades old, still burn with the intensity of that original emotion. Not only did I never learn to do the cartwheel but any form of dance or aerobics became a source of anxiety for me. You only have to recall one incident like this in your life to realise how destructive such open or mocking criticism is. The rule is ONLY PRAISE; whatever form or shape praise may take.

Praising a child, however, does not mean that you don't attempt to teach discipline or to set standards or boundaries. The child that has no structures or rules will be lost. The way that you explain the rules to the child is what counts. For example, 'I don't want you to

IT TOOK ME TWENTY YEARS BEFORE I CONFESSED TO MY PARENTS WHY, AT THE AGE OF FIVE, I RETURNED HOME EARLY FROM MY FIRST GYM CLASS IN MY NEW GYM CLOTHES AND SHOES, AND ANNOUNCED THAT I DID NOT LIKE IT AND WOULDN'T BE RETURNING.

run across the road without looking each way because I love you so much I couldn't bear for you to be hurt'.

Dawn French, the British comedy writer and actor, told Michael Parkinson the interviewer about her teenage years. She remembers one night when she was going to a disco. All her hormones were jumping and she said she was determined to bonk the first man with a pulse. Before she left, her father called her into his study and she expected the usual 'serious' talk. Instead he said, 'I want you to know that I think you are the most beautiful, the most gorgeous girl and because you are so precious to your mother and me I don't want you to just squander yourself on someone who isn't worthy of you'. After that she said anyone who even approached her that night was considered not good enough.

NEVER TELL A CHILD THAT THEY CAN'T DO SOMETHING. NEVER RIDICULE OR MOCK A CHILD'S EFFORTS. NEVER TELL A CHILD THAT THEY ARE STUPID. NEVER TELL A CHILD THAT THEY ARE HOPELESS.

Never tell a child that they can't do something. Never ridicule or mock a child's efforts. Never tell a child that they are stupid. Never tell a child that they are hopeless. And if you happen to spit these things out in anger, when you are calm tell them it was said in anger and that it wasn't true. Convince them of this by your future actions.

There are ways of giving criticism that are in fact a form of praise. The best teacher I ever had was also the most strict and the most critical. She made me stay behind after class for three weeks in a row, she made me weed the garden or sweep out the art room. In my early years, I was not a well-behaved student. I longed to leave school, get on the back of a motor bike behind my boyfriend, and ride off into the sunset. This teacher simply gave me no chance. She kept my nose to the grindstone by saying words like, 'I won't let you squander your talents'. In other words, she believed in me, even though I didn't.

Thirty years later she still writes to me to let me know she is following my latest adventure. And still the voice is one of praise; genuine, caring and sustaining. Fortunately for me an opportunity arose for me to thank her publicly and personally when I was asked to deliver the graduation address at my old high school. Afterwards she kept saying to me, 'Don't call me Mrs Palmer, Susan, call me Dawn. You are a woman now'. I said, 'Mrs Palmer, I could not possibly call you Dawn. You terrified me for too many years'. She thought my response was hilarious. Nor was my memory of my school record inaccurate. The current principal took me into her office and out of the dusty files of the past she took out my card and gave it to me. After I read it, all I could say was, 'Thank God for Miss Elliott and Mrs Palmer'. Teachers really do change lives.

Praise can appear in many guises, as long as we know it to be genuine. When I was teaching my creative writing classes at university, I noticed that the students had a great deal of trouble praising each other's work. When someone read out a mediocre piece of writing, the other students would try to say something good about it in a half-hearted way. When a student read out a truly excellent piece of work, however, there would be stunned silence and a showcase of downcast eyes and twisted faces. I finally confronted them with this and they were forced to admit that rather than praising the good writing, they were only thinking about the inadequacies of their own work and resenting the fact that theirs wasn't as good. At least admitting this openly was a start. Instead of repressing these feelings, I encouraged them to express them. 'Say what you really feel,' I persisted. And I made them speak what they had been hiding. The result was very liberating. The highest praise that anyone in the class could possibly receive was, 'You bastard, I hate you for writing so well'. The recipients of this statement would sail out of the class with huge grins on their faces, saying, 'They called me a bastard. Isn't that fantastic'. The other students would laugh as if it was a special secret that only that class shared.

We all envy someone else's talents but if you encourage people to express their envy honestly and openly, it will no longer control or own them. Only then can we get on with the task of not worrying about others but concentrating instead on doing better ourselves. Because creative writing is something that we view as an extension of ourselves, it is essential that a distinction be made between the content and the craft. When giving feedback on anything creative, it is important to try to remove the personal. Whenever a skill is being taught —like writing or tennis — much of the success or failure depends on keeping the feedback focused. For example, I always use the tennis analogy when teaching writing. Whenever the students start to take comments too personally, I say, 'Remember we're only talking about your backhand — not you'. Using this method ensures that any negative criticism is always seen in the framework of positive help.

Regardless of the subject area, all education should be focused on teaching students how to think, how to question, how to analyse. None of these skills will be transferred unless students feel confident that there is room to fail. Genuine confidence means that you will also be able to learn from the failure. Problem solving is the basis for most of our learning experiences.

Think back to the teachers who really made a difference to
  your life.
Think about the way they made you feel when they were
  teaching you.
Think about whether these were the subjects that you liked the
  most.
Think about whether these were the subjects in which you
  gained the best grades.
Think about whether this was a major influence in your choice
  of career.

If students believe that their parents or teachers have a genuine belief in their individual talents, whatever they are, then the students will make an effort to do their best.

*My first education was through correspondence
school, which I enjoyed. I used to run down and meet
the mailman, and then write back to my teacher.
We lived in the labourer's hut. Dad had to work
long hours for low wages. We were miles away from
the nearest family, but you have a lot of things
going for you when you live in the country. You
grow up with the sort of freedom that the city kids
don't have. There is a certain loneliness, and it's
harder for girls. Koorie mothers everywhere are
always frightened when there are white men
around. Since 1788 there's always been the pattern
of rape and exploitation of Koorie babies and little
girls. Even now in rural areas, all little Koorie girls
are taught not to go near white men.
My mother always talked to me about my culture,
which was important. When I was seven I went to
school in the city, and that's when the racism started
— being called, 'You dirty black bastard', and that
sort of thing. We had a very good headmaster, an
Englishman, who wouldn't countenance any racism.
My brother and I were the only Koorie kids in the
school, but fortunately for us we were very good at
sport. You know how sport is in Australia. We had
this little bunch of white groupies who used to
follow us around and bash up the other kids who
called us names.*

EVE FESL *Tall Poppies Too*

In terms of education, praise is both a trampoline and a safety net. It enables us to leap higher and also catches us when we fall. Whatever we learn in a lifetime of education is absorbed through a process of trial and error, success and failure. In order to embrace all knowledge with confidence and without the limitations of fear, we all need praise.

Margaret Mead, one of this century's most renowned anthropologists and celebrated teachers, said that the most important thing that we should teach children is 'To rest in the gale'. By that she meant 'being able to be at home anywhere in the world, in any house, in any time band, eating any different kind of food, learning new languages as needed, never afraid of the new, sad to leave anywhere one has been at home for a few days, but glad to go forward'. This is only possible if the child has a safety net of praise to make them feel confident and secure wherever they are or whatever they are confronting.

The main aim of education, whether someone is learning to cook, to play golf or music, is that you convince them that they can try new things and go further than they ever thought possible. To be told 'go for it' or 'give it a go' is, quite simply, high praise.

The safety net of praise helps us all to stretch and to dissolve our fear blocks. The best praise you can give someone who asks your opinion on whether they should try something new and expand themselves is, 'Of course it's possible. It has to be done and you alone can do it. What are you waiting for? Go for it'. The result is a surge of energy and purpose. You may think all this only applies to children but in the area of praise and recognition we are all children. Always. And a good teacher always reinforces the main points. Old habits die hard.

SUMMARY
1. Use praise to encourage at least one person to have a go at doing something they have always been afraid of. Encourage the person to make more mistakes faster.
2. Don't worry about fixed goals, as long as you are learning something.
3. Demystify formal learning.
4. Don't be afraid of competition but find something you can do really well.
5. Never ever tell anyone they are hopeless or stupid or rate them a zero.
6. Recognise when caring criticism is a form of praise.

7. It doesn't matter how you express praise, as long as it's genuine.
8. By encouraging people to express envy, you can release praise.
9. Divorce the teaching or learning of skills from the person.
10. Teach or learn the ability to 'rest in the gale'.

6

SELF: SEARCH FOR PRAISE

* Self-love
* Self-loathing
* Insecurity
* Creativity
* Humour

Before we can begin to deal with regenerating and improving our relationships with other people either personally or in the workplace, we have to take a long tough look at the relationship we have with ourselves.

Take yourself to a mirror or a mirror to yourself and stare hard at what you see. After you have inspected all your facial flaws and stopped being self-conscious about your appearance, experiment with saying your name to the person in the mirror three times. Say it the first time with no emotion, the second time with love and the third time with anger.

Now start a conversation with the person in the mirror that begins 'the problem with you is ...' and continue it for as long as you can.

Now start a conversation, still looking in the mirror, that begins, 'What I really like about you is ...' and continue it for as long as you can.

> *I love being an assertive, uppity woman. What's the*
> *alternative? The alternative is being depressed.*
> *There's no way to be a woman in this world and not*
> *be assertive and uppity unless you accept your*
> *oppression and just lie down and die or get into bed*
> *in the afternoon.*
> *You must be assertive and, in a way, I think it is*
> *very fortunate to be a woman in this sexist society.*
> *Just as it's fortunate in a way to be a Jew in an anti-*
> *Semitic world or a black in a racist world, because*
> *you're condemned to be the outsider and the outsider*
> *has a better vision of society than the insider.*
>
> ERICA JONG *Icons, Saints and Divas*

This is not an exercise in self-indulgence, it is simply stating openly, out loud, the kind of conversations you have silently, inside your head, with yourself several times a day.

After you have repeated this to the point of boredom, yes, you've guessed it. MAKE A LIST. In fact make two lists. One headed LIKE and the other LOATHE. Now go back to the mirror. Look at your face and smile.

> *I'm not a beauty and I'm not somebody who ever*
> *attracted men or women because I was the best-*
> *looking in the room. If I attracted people it was*
> *through sheer force of personality and because I'm*
> *in love with life. That comes across. I've known an*
> *awful lot of women who are not beauties who have*
> *men following after them like they're the universal*
> *honey pot. It's not just about what you look like. It's*
> *true that immature men at a certain age want to*

show off to the other guys that they can have a
model or whatever, but men who are a little bit
more mature want a woman who makes them feel
good about life and themselves.

ERICA JONG *Icons, Saints and Divas*

Now think of something that happened to you that really makes you want to smile or even laugh out loud. It doesn't matter what it is, visualise the person or the incident. Take a small page from a yellow 'post-it' pad and screw it up into a ball. This is a golden nugget of laughter. Place it in your pocket where it can't be seen but you can easily touch it with your hand or finger.

Now look in the mirror, touch your golden nugget of laughter and allow it to trigger the memory of laughter. Keep the golden nugget in a pocket every day for the next week and at least once a day purposely touch it and visualise the incident that makes you laugh. If this same incident ceases to produce the same result, then think of another one, make another golden nugget and repeat the process.

Giving yourself a secret moment in which to amuse yourself is a form of praise. It says that you deserve a nugget of laughter, not for any reason other than you are you.

A certain amount of self-love or like is essential if you are ever going to allow yourself to be bold enough to reach your potential.

Basically I have good features: I'm tall, all my
length is in my legs; if I'd been slim I would have
had a very good figure, and I would have been very
good-looking. But it didn't matter to me that I was
fat. If I had decided I wanted to make a living from
my face and figure, then I would have done
something about it. But that wasn't what I was
motivated to do.
The worst thing of all that happens to beautiful
women is that one day they grow old. My advice is:
hook yourself up to your brain, whatever you're

doing. What I have achieved does not depend on
how I look.

COLLEEN MCCULLOUGH *Tall Poppies Too*

If, however, you are often consumed by a secret dislike or even loathing for yourself because you believe that you have let yourself down or never achieved what you believe you should have, then one thing is certain — you never will. Self-loathing is in itself a self-fulfilling prophecy. And what you have seeded in your head will show in your face.

By practising these small habits, which are easily accessible, any time of the day or night, you actually begin to change the dialogue you are consciously or unconsciously having with yourself. As a result, your self-loathing will, like the seed that gets no water, food or sunshine, gradually wither and die.

The aim here is not to turn yourself into a self-absorbed egomaniac but to somehow find a balance between the love and the loathing, so that each holds the other in check.

Basically I do believe in myself very much, and
believe that the turns that I take are all terrific ones.
I'm very instinctual. The happiest moments are
when I'm sitting at the computer and good stuff's
coming out, and I think everything I've done so far
has come from the right decisions.
If you want to succeed you have to look to yourself.
I just wish creative stuff wasn't squashed out of
everyone. That's what I wish. I wish people weren't
in boring jobs, and I wish society wasn't constructed
so that people have to spend their time so uselessly.
My success has come as an adjunct to being honest
about what I wanted to do.
When everything finally came together I found a
way to be the best that I could possibly be, on stage
or off. I finally did things with a full heart, with

complete passion, and people enjoyed this. Now
there is no dichotomy.
The people who succeed will continue to be the
people who really remain true to themselves. I've
always believed that I've had a spectacularly good
time and great success, but really I can't hold that
I'm inherently better to do that than anybody else.

ROBYN ARCHER *Tall Poppies Too*

So many books tell you that you must first learn to love yourself before you can possibly love anyone else, but that is not strictly true. You can develop a totally independent, all-consuming, obsessive love for someone else in order to forget or assuage your basic disappointment with yourself. The whole basis of 'romantic love' is that you lose yourself in the other person. You dissolve or merge into them. This involves a loss of self and thereby allows you to remove yourself from any responsibility for either the relationship or any suffering it causes you. The aim of self-love is to ensure that when you do love someone else you don't lose yourself.

How are things going at the moment for you? Are they going well? Are you taking the credit for this? Are you enjoying it? Or scared that it won't last?

Whenever things are going right, most of us think to ourselves, 'I must be on a lucky streak' and keep our fingers crossed that it will last. Whenever things go wrong we think, 'I knew I'd stuff it up'. In other words we never take the credit or praise ourselves for the good things but always berate ourselves for the bad. Whenever things are going either really well or really badly we must pay special attention to what is being said inside our heads. If you hear a voice beating you up then go straight to the mirror and look at your face. It will probably not be generating sunshine. (It may even look like something painted by Edward Munch.)

If you are reading this during what is a tough time for you, then you are probably thinking, 'Oh all this mirror rubbish is all very well, but you don't know what it's like'.

Well, no, I probably don't know the words but I could hum the tune. Anyone who has ever tried and failed, or made themselves vulnerable and been rejected, as indeed I have, knows what rejection feels like. Some of us block the hurt and anger, some of us bury it and some of us feed on it. Those who take it on board as experience and move on, perhaps only to have it happen again, but continue to pick themselves up and keep going, are people that we recognise as successes or winners. Those who give up and never try again are the real losers.

> *Nothing in life is ever wasted. If there is a God, I know only one thing about him. He hates a quitter. He'll forgive murder ahead of quitting. Life is a gift meant to be used wisely and well. So you keep on trying to make the best of it. You don't give up, and you don't give in.*
>
> COLLEEN MCCULLOUGH *Tall Poppies Too*

We all have awful experiences at some stages in our lives, some of which we cause, some we have absolutely no control over. Not too many escape, do they? One way or another. It's how we decide to deal with these negative experiences that really counts. What you say to yourself during these periods forms the basis for what kind of future you will have. If you wallow in your bad fortune or beat yourself up over your failings, you will simply extend the pain.

So often the internal conflict — the battle between your best self and your worst self, your productive, energetic, motivated self and your lazy, lethargic, drifting self — is the hardest one of all to deal with. During the writing of this book I have constantly been blocked. Not because I don't know what to write or I don't believe in what I am writing but because I lacked confidence in my credentials to write such a book. The conflict inside my head goes something like this. I'm not a psychologist or a psycho-therapist, nor am I a professional motivator or self-help guru. Who am I to take this on? Here I am writing a book on the power of praise and being bold and I'm constantly crippled with self-doubt, seized up with the fear of making a fool of myself. Days go by and I write nothing. I'm suddenly so tired I can't physically sit at the desk. If I try to do some research I fall asleep on the couch. It's avoidance, I know. But I'm paralysed. I talk to my friends. They say, 'But it's precisely because you are not any of those things that is the book's strength. You have been a teacher, a lecturer, a communicator, a broadcaster and this is what you have learned. It's simple, straight-forward and powerful'. Yes, yes, but perhaps it's too simple. Then I say, stop beating yourself up, Susan. What is all this negative thinking? Flick the switch to the positive channel. Practise what you preach.

I go to the doctor. 'Are you depressed?' he asks me. 'Well, yes, in a way. I'm overweight, not doing enough exercise because I'm sitting at my desk not writing enough. I have a deadline and I'm so tired. I just want to sleep all the time.'

So I agree to have some blood tests. Perhaps I need some Prozac? Something to increase the levels of serotonin. Praise is better than Prozac. You know that. Stop being so hard on yourself. You have never missed a deadline. You will make this one. Just sit down and write. Now. And I do. Finally. But when I start the next chapter I go through it all again. Most writers will recognise this conflict. It is certainly not confined to me but with every book I keep thinking it will get easier. It doesn't.

Somehow I tap into the confidence to keep going. I don't ring my agent and tell him I can't finish the book or I'll have to pay back the advance. (That's always a motivating factor as I've usually spent it.) Somehow I stop beating myself up for not being the disciplined, motivated, organised person I plan to become and drag my old, battered, imperfect self back to the desk. I talk to myself like the tennis player who is two sets all and five love down. I say, 'You can do this. You've done it before. Just concentrate on the positive. Don't worry about the score. Just do the best you can'.

Question: How do you eat an elephant?

Answer: One bite at a time.

And so one page at a time I urge myself on. And gradually, in bursts and fits, the book is written. You must be your own coach. Just keep telling yourself that you can do it. That you will get there.

When you are failing to live up to your own standards, lower your standards. Perhaps you are expecting too much from yourself. Perhaps you expect too much from other people. Particularly those you love.

We are all afraid that we are not good enough at whatever we choose to do or be. This fear of failure is what is at the bottom of perfectionism. The notion that if only you had tried harder or been better at it, is the creed of the perfectionist. So often we give up something that we enjoy doing, simply because we don't think we do it well enough. We make our own lives a misery because of this standard of perfection against which we measure ourselves. Simply doing the best you can, at a particular time and place, ought to be enough. But, we keep asking ourselves, was it really my best? And of course we don't merely impose these standards of perfectionism on ourselves, we use them as the measuring stick for everyone else, especially those we love. Being tough and critical on ourselves leads us to be likewise with others. It also leads us to be mean with praise and rewards or the withholder of the same as a form of punishment. And so the cycle is repeated with your children.

THE DAY THAT YOU DECIDE TO ALLOW YOURSELF TO BE IMPERFECT, TO FORGIVE YOURSELF YOUR IMPERFECTIONS, TO FORGIVE OTHERS THEIRS, IS THE DAY YOU DECIDE JUST TO BE HUMAN.

Perfectionists have a hellish life. And they are hell to live with. The day that you decide to allow yourself to be imperfect, to forgive yourself your imperfections, to forgive others theirs, is the day you decide just to be human. You will have a happier life, so will those around you. That doesn't mean that you don't strive to do your best, but don't beat yourself up by making your best a perfect score.

So many people have childhood stories about when they really tried hard and came third or fifth and when they took their report cards home to their parents, instead of the praise that they expected, they were told, 'never mind, you'll do better next time' or 'who came first?'

Everyone makes mistakes, everyone fails to live up to the standards they have set themselves. Those who are successful in the real sense, give themselves credit for having tried hard rather than criticism for having failed to reach perfection.

A lot of the words that are in your head have been planted there by parents or teachers long before you even realised what they were doing. There is no point in blaming them for planting weeds and not flowers. If you take possession of a house which has a preponderance of weeds you don't waste time blaming the previous owners, you simply set about getting rid of them. You know that if you allow the weeds to flourish they will take over and kill off everything else. If your head is a weed-choked garden, then simply decide that you will get rid of the weeds and plant your own flowers. Be aware of course that once weeds are in the soil, they can easily return. Every time you see one, pull it out by the roots and plant a flower in its place. Every time you have a negative thought, don't just block it, replace it with a positive thought. Visualise it as a weed, pull it out by the roots and plant one of your favourite flowers there. Every night before you go to sleep, particularly if you are starting on that long journey of worrying and insomnia, visualise your garden and focus on all the flowers that you have planted there. If necessary, rip out a few weeds and plant some more flowers.

But what if, no matter how hard you try, your facial expression gives you away? You just aren't one of those people who can mask your real feelings. Recently one of my friends whose father was about to undergo a very serious operation rang me to ask for help. 'He may die during the operation but the doctor said it's very important that we keep him positive and don't let the fear show in our faces. How do I do this? Every time I look at his darling old face I nearly burst into tears at the thought that I might never see him again.' I told her to imagine that she had a television set in her head and that she could switch from one channel to another. Whenever her head switched onto the worry or the fear channel she had to immediately flick the remote to another station, preferably the one that showed home movies of all the good times they had shared together. At least then when she looked at him her face would be smiling and shining through the tears.

Even better, I told her, is to flick the switch to the family comedy channel. There are always incidents you remember, particularly with your parents, when your actions vastly amused you, but not necessarily them. One of my favourites with my father occurred over dinner when a cousin and I were playing around with a sauce bottle and generally being silly ten year olds. Eventually my father could stand it no longer. He leant across the table and seized the bottle. Unfortunately for him, it was the soft squeezy variety and the force with which he grabbed it caused the sauce to project itself in a clear red line across his head and his nose. He just sat there. Totally still and without a flicker of emotion. He looked like Chief Sitting Bull in full war paint. My cousin and I screamed with laughter and could not stop. Even my mother cracked up. My father simply stood up and without a glimmer of a smile walked slowly out of the dining room towards the bathroom. To this day I still laugh aloud when I visualise him sitting there with his head decorated with the sauce.

WHENEVER HER HEAD SWITCHED ONTO THE WORRY OR THE FEAR CHANNEL SHE HAD TO IMMEDIATELY FLICK THE REMOTE TO ANOTHER STATION, PREFERABLY THE ONE THAT SHOWED HOME MOVIES OF ALL THE GOOD TIMES THEY HAD SHARED TOGETHER.

I know that you have similar incidents that you can put in your comedy channel and watch whenever you press the play button.

My friend rang a week after her father's operation to say that she and her mother had practised flicking from the negative to the positive television channels in their heads. She said they were so successful that when her father was being wheeled into surgery he was so cheerful he not only kissed them but insisted on kissing the nurse as well. Of course they wept once he had disappeared from view but he came through a very long and difficult operation. Afterwards he told them how much he appreciated their courage, their humour and their belief in him.

Humour and smiling are very important in our lives. Imagine how long you would watch a presenter on television if they constantly scowled at you. In fact no-one would maintain a job in the visual media if they never smiled. I'm not speaking here of a false smile; that fools no-one. It is interesting to monitor how often and when you smile during a day. A genuine smile, the kind that lights up a face and sometimes a room, can only come from within.

> *Our fish and chips got really famous in a short time. The manager of Kellogg's at that time, a Mr Roach, an American, rang me up and said 'I want a table'. And I said, 'We don't book any tables, we haven't got the room. You'll just have to come and wait in the queue with the rest of the people'. Jack was cooking in the kitchen when Mr Roach came in, and said, 'Where's my table?' He'd had a few, I think. I said, 'I told you, we haven't got one'. He said 'You know what you can do with your fish?' And I said 'You can do the same with your cornflakes and don't forget the banana'. Everybody was treated the same.*
>
> ALICE DOYLE *The Matriarchs*

A person's smile will tell you exactly the kind of relationship that someone has with themself. A smile is a form of praise, both to yourself and other people.

If you realise that you don't in fact give a real smile very often in a day, then you need to take some action to change that. Sometimes you can trick yourself into it and having consciously practised the habit for a few days, it will become part of you. One of the side effects of going through a really rough patch in your life is that you are often unaware that you are frequently frowning. If you are in a meeting, look around the table and assess the expression on each person's face. I am certainly not suggesting that you practise sitting in meetings with a silly grin on your face, but you probably don't realise when your brow is furrowed.

It wasn't until someone said to me, 'why are you often frowning?' that I monitored that my brow was always creased whenever I was thinking. If you are attempting to persuade other people to follow or support you in a bold move or change of direction, your task will be much harder if you don't look relaxed and therefore confident.

We are all fearful that the things that we most want to achieve in our personal or professional lives will not happen because we will let ourselves down. It is so much easier to blame others or institutional barriers for our shortcomings. In some instances it is necessary to undertake legal proceedings but our own fear of failure is often a major factor. This inner fear reflects itself in insecure behaviour which will make it harder for us to succeed. We have to get rid of the fear.

BBC television made a program about a group of people who could not shake off what could loosely be described as mild depression or melancholia. Each person finally came to the realisation that this had become their dominant feeling and that their relationship with themselves was closer to a frown than a smile. It seemed impossible to them that they would ever be able to change. They had lost their verve or perhaps some of them had never known how to tap into it. They allowed themselves to be retrained in the habit of smiling, laughing and being secure in those feelings as a way of life. The documentary cameras followed each of them through the six-week course and by the end of it most of them were smiling and all were a great deal less melancholic than when they started. A scientist measured the areas of the brain that dealt with their depression and there was definitely a positive change that could be scientifically measured. The course proved that you can teach yourself or be taught to change the relationship with yourself. No wonder large sections of the Western world are on Prozac or some other form of antidepressant, chemical or herbal. It is clearly a lot easier to allow a substance to release serotonin in the brain than to work on techniques which allow us to trigger it in ourselves. But how much better not to be reliant on anything external.

Research psychologist Martin Seligman, of the University of Pennsylvania, believes that one's view of life, either optimistic or pessimistic, affects health, life expectancy and success. In his recent book *Learned Optimism* he sets out twenty years of evidence for his claims.

Pessimism and depression have risen rapidly since the Second World War, with young people ten times more likely to suffer severe depression than their grandparents. He says that pessimists attribute bad events, such as the loss of a job or the breakup of a marriage, to causes that are pervasive, long-lasting or permanent and always their own fault; whereas optimists see the causes of such events as temporary, limited to the present case and the result of circumstances, bad luck or other people's actions. Pessimists see success as luck; optimists as a result of their own skill and efforts.

> *I don't feel anything about fame, to me it's just an illusion. It's not something I take seriously at all. What matters to me is the quality of my work. I wrote for twenty years, sending novels and stories out, and I got rejected for twenty years. For twenty years the world of publication told me I was no good. The last fifteen they've been telling me I'm good. I can't believe one any more than I believed the other. I could only trust myself, I could only believe in myself.*
> MARILYN FRENCH *Icons, Saints and Divas*

Dr Seligman believes that both optimism and pessimism are learned in childhood. When children fail, the criticism of both parents and teachers has a big impact. This of course supports my theory in this book about the power of praise in our lives as opposed to the destructive effects of criticism. Dr Seligman's research shows that if children fail a test and then hear a 'permanent and pervasive' criticism, such as 'you are stupid or no good', then this becomes part of what they believe about themselves. But if the response explains that problems are solvable and specific, then that is how they see them.

Overcoming negative thinking takes work and practice, but Dr Seligman believes optimism is easy to maintain once you have learned the habit. He suggests recognising the automatic negative thoughts that enter your head when things go wrong. They can rapidly become negative beliefs, determining how you feel and act. In the beginning he says it helps to write them down. Then the crucial step is to rationally dispute them with yourself. We don't hesitate to defend a loved one against other people's attacks but fail to do the same for ourselves against our own self-criticisms.

> *I'm very optimistic and confident that I am on the right pathway wherever I am; whatever happens, it's going to be all right. Life's not always comfortable, but I think, 'This is just a bit of a dip, and it will be revealed to you what it's all about'. I can't say that I always sail through and think, 'I'm wonderful. Everything's going wonderfully'. Clearly it's not like that.*
>
> ROBYN ARCHER *Tall Poppies Too*

Dr Seligman's technique is different from the more generalised method of positive thinking, such as saying to yourself 'every day, in every way, I'm getting better and better'. He says that if you can actually believe such statements then more power to you, but that many educated people trained in sceptical thinking cannot. His method of learned optimism is based on accuracy. For example, you may think that your exam results were the worst in the class, but if you check the evidence you will probably find that they were not. He also suggests distracting yourself from negative thoughts by writing them down and addressing them later.

Mild pessimism, however, can sometimes have its uses 'by pulling us back from rash, foolhardy gestures'. Psychologist John Dibley, who conducts study seminars for high school students, says optimistic thinking only helps people if it is realistic and motivates them to act. He says there is a big difference between positive thinking and self-delusion. There is no point in saying 'I'm feeling hot' if you are feeling cold. He would prefer that someone says 'I'm feeling cold but I can handle it'.

He points out that one of the problems of the traditional 'positive thinking' ideology is that it suggests that all you have to do is think something and it will happen. Students may learn positive thinking but they also need study skills. The two are part of a package. But he does believe that students and adults who are optimistic and think positively are 'more likely to get off their butts and make their expectations a reality'.

If you want to be really good at anything you have to be very single-minded. You have to make up your mind whether you are going to do it properly, which means giving up a lot of things and not having people distracting you from your agenda and dragging you into theirs, because otherwise you'll never succeed. Sport taught me that, if I wanted to improve enough to make the state team and win a championship, I just had to go and train. When other girls went off to dances or with boys I put on my tracksuit, picked up my discus or my javelin or my spikes, and went training.

I had to work to get to the top. My brother had it naturally, and you'll find that lots of young people who are very good at sport and get it so easy when they are very young don't become the top people. Too much too soon, and too easy. You get to a stage where natural ability won't get you there; you just

have to put the work in, develop the techniques and
the expertise.

EVE FESL *Tall Poppies Too*

I am quoting psychologists not because I think my theory about praise is shaky, but because, like many things that you instinctively know to be true, science provides the necessary evidence.

Just to be optimistic, to do your best to banish negative thoughts and replace them with positive ones, is a form of praise.

I see myself as much more than a survivor. Much
more. Because in my life there is a lot of joy and,
again, I think that when you just survive there's a
good feeling about that, but the best feeling of all is
to really feel at home on the planet, connected to it
in a way that is all yours. I do feel that. I have
always felt that way.

ALICE WALKER *Icons, Saints and Divas*

Praise in all its guises is the beginning of starting to improve the relationship that you have with yourself. What kinds of conversations do you have with yourself inside your head or even aloud?

What do you say when you do something stupid?
What do you say when you do something clever?
What do you say when you find yourself in a difficult
   situation?
Do you have an innate belief that you can deal with anything?

If, for example, you were to imagine yourself in some form of extreme deprivation, like people who were interned in a concentration camp during the Second World War, what would you be saying to yourself?

> *There is a wonderful book,* Man's Search for
> Meaning, *by Victor Frankel. As a German Jew he*
> *spent six or seven years in Auschwitz and Sachau.*
> *He writes about how he survived that environment*
> *and, more importantly, as an informed observer,*
> *how he saw other people survive. He said that if life*
> *has a 'why' and you know why you are doing what*
> *you are doing and why you live, then no matter*
> *how you find yourself, where you find yourself, you*
> *will prosper.*
>
> FABIAN DATTNER, *Tall Poppies Too*

Fabian Dattner inherited her family's successful business and expanded it into her dream company. Renowned for her work with prisoners and her establishment of the Second Chance Scheme to help them gain employment after leaving prison, no-one but herself could help her when her company fell victim to economic recession. What is extraordinary is the way she dealt with what happened and how she managed to reframe her experience in order to gain some positive value from it. She now advises people as a keynote speaker and a facilitator on how to go about turning adversity into opportunity.

Gloria Steinem is the most famous feminist of our time. In my book, *Icons, Saints and Divas*, which tells the inside story of the ten days I spent trekking the steamy streets of New York talking to the top ten US women writers, Gloria told me about the worst period of her life.

> *Fifty-five was a time of great momentous change for*
> *me. I had hit the bottom of the swimming pool some*
> *time in my early fifties, and I was just beginning to*
> *come back up again. When you've been under great*
> *pressure you only realise it hurts when you stop.*
> *There were lots of causes. The pressure of the*
> *magazine, losing the magazine, breast cancer, age,*

*exhaustion. All those things came together. It was
very tough. There were a lot of months when the
world for me was no longer in colour, it was black
and white. But I've always thought of myself as a
survivor. I have always had the belief that if there
were only a few people left in the concentration camp
I want to be one of them. But I really had lost my
optimism and my energy and my ability to look
forward. I was a very non-introspective person. I
had really neglected my own version of 'the personal
is political'. Like many of us, I looked at the politics
of my present life but not at the politics of my
growing up. I had to get rid of the brick wall with
which I had sealed off my early years. I didn't
realise that they were continuing to influence my life.*

SPAN GLORIA STEINEM *Icons, Saints and Divas*

George Stephanopoulos was in his early thirties when he became President Bill Clinton's Press Secretary and the 'face' of the president at White House briefings. When, however, the president decided to put someone else in his job and give him the nebulous title of Senior Advisor for Policy and Strategy, he had to face the cameras as the president told the world of his demotion.

The touchstone for his behaviour was a piece of advice from a former congressman who told him, 'Nobody will remember what happened to you. But they'll remember how you handle it'.

There is always a solution to any problem you have, there is always a way of negotiating an impasse but you have to free yourself to approach your life more creatively in order to find it.

Edward de Bono has made a career out of writing, speaking and teaching people how to approach problems by thinking creatively or, as he says, laterally. It is impossible, however, to even begin to think creatively unless you first deal with your relationship with yourself. If you think of your brain as a version of the internet where you can click onto anything you wish, then your imagination becomes the search engine. Surfing the net becomes a way of surfing your mind. Just let it click onto dream wishes. I now realise that when teachers used to accuse me of wasting time in class by daydreaming, I was in fact using the search engine in my own mind.

Instead of sitting in front of the computer, use at least half of that time to sit or lie quietly, and just allow yourself to click onto your own mind. You will find a www that will amaze and delight you.

Go back to your very first list and check those things that you said you would really like to achieve. Take them one by one and set some time aside to daydream about them or visualise yourself in that role.

First, allow your mind to play creatively with anything that comes to mind. Don't try to control it, just let it click onto whatever image or word it chooses. But make sure that you always place yourself in the centre of every scenario.

Anything that you achieve in your life or any role that you succeed in playing will inevitably be something that you have seen yourself doing in your imagination, if only for a secret moment.

Dare to daydream. Or just before you drift off to sleep at night, allow yourself to be or do whatever you wish and hug it close to yourself. Creativity is not just about writing books or music, or painting pictures. They are just the end products of allowing yourself to surf the www of your imagination. To allow yourself time to do this is recognition that time spent in your own head is time worth spending.

The only danger is that you will find that your imagination is so much fun that you may prefer it to the so-called 'real' world of the day to day. It is important to focus on one of the items on your wish list and not merely slip into a dream world as a means of never doing anything. Just as you may plant the seed in the ground, you still have to actively water, fertilise and weed in order for it to grow and ultimately flower. This takes discipline and mental toughness.

Sports psychologists are now seen as equally important as sports coaches. In individual sports such as swimming or golf, winning requires extraordinary mental toughness. This means teaching people to think about their thinking. If basically you are what you think you are, then giving people the tools with which they can motivate themselves is the first step.

Most of the techniques are standard and the jargon self-explanatory.

'Visualisation' is really just imagining yourself doing something.

'Positive self-talk' means concentrating on what you can do rather than what you can't.

One of the more popular techniques employed in order to teach athletes to get rid of negative thoughts and focus on the positive is the use of 'cue' words. The most obvious words for athletes to use are 'power' or 'smooth' or 'relax', but often it's individual esoteric words that work best.

For example, Clark Perry, sports psychologist at the Australian Institute of Sport, worked on one particular athlete's technique for months and months, and suddenly one day noticed that his stroke was perfect. He stopped him right at that moment and said, 'What are you thinking about?' The athlete said, 'Actually I'm thinking about avocados and a conversation I had with my girlfriend'. So when he swam, avocados became his cue word because it caused him to relax and relaxation improved his stroke.

This technique can be used by anyone. Just find a cue word that makes you focus or feel confident or relaxed or positive and whenever you find yourself thinking negative thoughts use your cue word.

'Affirmations' are just another form of self-praise, and are also very popular with sports psychologists. They usually consist of a simple phrase like 'I am a powerful swimmer' and they are always stated in the positive and always in the present. Even if you do not always believe it to be true, you must say it to yourself as if it is true.

Clark Perry believes that 'one of the things that tends to bring most of us down is our own negative language. We never really see the good qualities within us. Affirmations are a good way of getting us to break down those barriers of negativity that prevent us from achieving our best'.

Basically all the techniques used by sports psychologists can be applied to everyday living, particularly when you are under stress. No-one in the world has been under more public pressure than President Bill Clinton and yet what has been remarkable and extraordinary has been his ability to get on with his job and really look as if he is not weighed down by his problems or his enemies. He is a perfect example of someone who has developed techniques which enable him to block out the negative thoughts and concentrate on the positive, even when the eyes of the world are upon him.

Perhaps his friend, the golfer Greg Norman, has given him a few tips. What is generally considered to be amazing about Norman is his ability to pull himself out of slumps. The American motivator, Anthony Robbins, pointed out that most people have one or two 'light switches' — ways of getting their concentration back on their game whereas Norman has about 30.

WE ARE ALL CONSTANTLY BATTLING NEGATIVITY IN OUR OWN MINDS WHICH IS WHY WE NEED ALL THE HELP WE CAN GET. BUT ALL THE SPORTS PSYCHOLOGY IN THE WORLD HAS TO BE MATCHED WITH HARD WORK.

International golfer, Ian Baker-Finch, admitted in a recent *60 Minutes* interview that his self-described fear of embarrassing himself, of failing to live up to expectations, was at one point so crippling that he lost all confidence in his game. He said, 'It was almost impossible for me, as hard as I tried, to dream good thoughts or to visualise hitting straight drives'.

We are all constantly battling negativity in our own minds, which is why we need all the help we can get. But all the sports psychology in the world has to be matched with hard work. Having done the visualisation, the positive self-talk, the cue word, the affirmation, an athlete still has to plough the pool, a golfer work on the swing, a tennis player practise the serve. So too a writer has to craft the words, a pianist hit the keys, an artist slap the paint. As Clark Perry says, 'The essence of it all is to forget about winning but not to forget about how to play and win'.

The aim of this chapter is to give you the skills with which to motivate yourself in order to best prepare yourself mentally. And as with every skill, you have to constantly practise it. Unlike the woman who said to one of the world's best concert pianists, 'I suppose now that you are this good you don't have to practise so hard'. If only it was true.

7

OTHERS: PRAISE A LOT AND OFTEN

* Love
* Fear
* Frustration
* Loneliness
* Rejection

Do you praise those you love at least once a day?
Do you say just one thing that will make them feel good about
  themselves?
If you don't, why not?
Are you bold enough to make your love work?

How many forests have been felled in the writing of books and
articles in an attempt to make sense of, to find some pathway
towards succeeding in our personal relationships?

Love with a capital 'L' and its pursuit has absorbed more of our
waking and sleeping hours than most of us would care to admit. And
why not? To love and be loved in return is the most satisfying and

sublime emotion that we as humans can experience. Of course it is what we all openly or secretly desire. Those who say they don't have these desires have either given up, lost all hope or are in deep denial.

Whatever our sexual preferences or proclivities, underlying them all is the same genderless need for the kind of warmth and security that comes from the knowledge that you share this special 'love' feeling with another human being. The search for this is usually fraught with false trails, dead-ends and all kinds of misinformation, unless you miraculously find someone when you are young and manage to sustain your love as it grows and changes with age. Most of us bumble and stumble along as if lost in the bush, desperately hoping that someone will rescue us before we die of thirst or starvation or deprivation (or depravity).

Amazingly these someones usually cross our paths. Sometimes we don't recognise them for who they are or will become. The best stories told by lovers are those where one or both of them had no idea of the other's importance when they first stumbled across each other's lives.

Eventually one of them is hit by the realisation of love and is bold enough to demonstrate or even declare the intensity of their feelings. Or perhaps they don't, ever. And like the two characters in the film *The Remains of the Day* played by Emma Thompson and Anthony Hopkins, the moment will pass them by. By the time the two of them finally get around to meeting each other it is too late. Had one of these characters been bold enough to declare their love, the entire course of their lives would have been changed. Of course this film was set in pre-war Britain when repression and reticence were signs of proper behaviour. Even though we have all become a lot more free with our bodies since then, I'm not sure that we are necessarily more courageous in being the first to declare our love.

For to do so is fraught with danger. And danger generates fear, even terror. Fear of making yourself vulnerable, fear of being embarrassed, of being hurt or rejected, or worst of all of being ignored. There is a poignant if hilarious scene in the television series *Seinfeld* where the character of chubby, bald George decides he will tell the girl he has been dating that he loves her. Jerry Seinfeld, his best friend and confidante, cautions him against doing this on the grounds that once you actually say the words 'I love you' it really places you out there on a limb. If the person doesn't reciprocate then the cradle breaks and crashing down you go 'cradle and all'. The winds of rejection and indifference are fierce and unforgiving. Undeterred, George screws up his courage, declares his love and the girl ignores him. He is shattered. But a few days later when he realises that she is in fact deaf in one ear, he tries again. Her only response is, 'I heard you the first time'. This is of course black humour.

For in truth, to declare one's love, either romantic or platonic, is the highest form of praise. When someone of any age or gender looks you in the eye and says, 'I want you to know that I love you' it's always a knock-out sensation.

Sometimes it takes us by surprise and we don't know how to respond so we say nothing ... or giggle ... or look away ... or mumble something pathetic. Why, when all our lives we seek so desperately to be loved, do we so often hurt someone by not knowing how to receive it?

If someone gave you a beautifully wrapped birthday or Christmas present and you took it and put it aside or never opened it or even if you did take it but never commented on it, wouldn't you think this was despicable behaviour? And yet a declaration of love is probably the best present you will ever receive (give or take the odd Mercedes or diamond cluster).

When we are little we think nothing of sitting on our father's lap playing with his hair or snuggling up to our mother and saying 'I love you'. We write gaudy cards with totally over-the-top illustrations and exclamations, and hand them over to our loved ones with no self-consciousness. We are bold in our declarations. Somehow, somewhere most of us lose this boldness. Now is the time to find it and reclaim it. Today I want you to either say or write 'I love you' (on a golden nugget post-it) to someone you love whom you have never said it to or at least not for a long time. It doesn't matter what kind or flavour of love it is as long as it's honestly felt. In doing this you must promise that you won't let your fear stop you. And even if you pick up the phone, blurt it out and hang up with red cheeks flaming with embarrassment, do not regret that you were bold enough to do it. For in that act of boldness, you have begun to liberate yourself and in that act of liberation you have already begun to live more fully and to open yourself up to opportunities for further self-expression.

Once when I was a student teacher, one of the older so-called spinster teachers on the staff confessed to me in a rash moment that she had recently declared her love for a much younger man. At that stage in my life I remember thinking 'how stupid, he would never be interested in someone like you and all you have done is make a fool of yourself'. Certain of what I was thinking and before I could frame a suitably euphemistic response she said, 'I'm glad I did it. I feel free of it now. Of course it will lead to nothing but I wanted him to know, to accept it freely as a gift'. I doubted that the young man in question was worthy of such a generous gift, but it is not until you experience unrequited love that you realise that you can free yourself with an act of boldness.

Too often it seems we wait until the person is dying or very ill or in some kind of desperate state before we tell them that we love them or admire them or value them highly. Marilyn French recounts an incident in her memoir *A Season in Hell* which documents her fight and final victory over cancer, where just prior to her having chemotherapy a friend asked to come over for a drink. Marilyn was surprised because even though they read each other's books and had dinner together a few times a year this woman was not the one who initiated their meetings. Over a drink in Marilyn's study the woman told her that she knew she was very sick and that people often fail to say important things to each other before it was too late. She went on to say that she wanted to tell Marilyn, while she was alive, that she loved her.

> *I imagined that professing loving friendship might*
> *be difficult for her. So I was especially grateful for*
> *her words, for her courage in uttering them and her*

generosity in making the effort. And that she felt
loving toward me pleased me. I cared about her as
well, I said. Her act was one of the more moving
events of this period, and I will never forget it.

It is a common but sad commentary on what it takes before people are prepared to overcome their fears and express their true feelings. It's never too late.

As the character that Walter Matthau plays in *Out to Sea* says, 'There's no such thing as too late, that's why they invented death'.

So make a list. As you know, I'm big on lists. I would never get through the day, let alone the supermarket, without a list. I am too easily distracted and waylaid. Lists focus the mind.

Make a list *now* of all the people that you can honestly say you love, whatever form or flavour it takes. Don't think about whether they love you. Don't think about what their reaction might be. Just promise yourself that day by day, in your own way, you will tell them so, boldly. And then cross their names off the list to check up on yourself.

If you are one of the fortunate people who is never afraid to tell people that you love them, don't stop now. To feel love in all its myriad and sometimes contradictory forms is to know that you are alive. To be able to express it is to know that you are fully alive. The late Elizabeth Riddell at the end of what was a long, intimate and courageously honest interview in *Tall Poppies* replied when asked about what she loved, 'My loves? Love. That's all'.

If loving someone is the highest form of praise then conversely praising them is a kind of love that we can give each other. We forget that to say 'I love you' is only a beginning. In order to say those three small words openly and honestly, we know that if we really analyse it, there are many aspects of that loved person that you could praise. Remember real praise is specific and personal.

In the Oscar award winning film *As Good As It Gets*, the Helen Hunt character, an exhausted mother and waitress, says to the Jack Nicholson character, a mean-mouthed, compulsive-disordered romance writer, 'Pay me a compliment'. This is the hardest thing for this selfish, self-obsessed, dysfunctional man to do. After some difficulty he says, 'You make me want to be a better man'. She is delighted by this but then he wrecks it all and she tells him that she doesn't want to know him because he doesn't make her feel good about herself. In a last desperate attempt to save their relationship and salvage his life, he goes over to her house at 4 a.m. And in a classic example of the power of praise, he talks to her.

He tells her he has a great compliment to pay her; that he could be the only person on earth who appreciates how incredible she is in everything she does. That she says what she means and practically always means something that's about being 'straight and good', something many people miss about her. He watches her customers, wondering how they can see her waiting on them and never realise they just met 'the greatest woman alive'. However, the fact that he understands it makes him feel good about himself.

Then he boldly kisses her. The power of his praise has released him. And her. 'It blesseth him that gives and him that takes' (to paraphrase from Portia's view of mercy in *The Merchant of Venice*).

Our failure to express love or praise to people with whom we have personal relationships is often based on a sense of frustration that we feel about our own lives.

When we feel that our own efforts are not being rewarded or recognised, particularly by those closest to us, we close ourselves off from rewarding or recognising the achievements or attributes of others. We may notice when someone does something kind or generous or praiseworthy but a voice inside our head, a mean little voice, says, 'That's the least they can do'.

And yet so often our frustration with the ways that our personal relationships fail to please or satisfy us is the very mechanism which cements or locks people into positions from which they find it so hard to extricate themselves.

So make another list. This time a list of all the personal relationships that you find frustrating. You may of course discover that it has many of the same names that you placed on the people you love list. Funny that.

One of the catalysts for releasing frustration is to give the person who is really getting under your skin some form of praise. With someone that you know well, try experimenting with small comments like, 'I've always liked that colour dress (shirt, suit) on you'. Note the person's reaction. Gradually, like turning up the volume on a piece of music, get bolder, more personal, more direct until finally you will find that actually you do find qualities in them that you admire. You will also find that the frustration that you felt has gradually melted away in your efforts to look for the positive and express it. You may even find that some of that praise has bounced back on you. Praise is like a boomerang once you put enough energy into pitching it high. It will always return to you.

Whatever it is that you need, you must first of all give it freely. This is of course the 'you reap what you sow' parable and I firmly believe in it. If what you feel people never give you is recognition for your work, then you must first of all give it to someone else. If life is not delivering to you what you really want from it, then you must look closely at what you are giving to others in your life.

Those who are mean spirited in any way will receive very little generosity. And the meaner and tighter you become, so too the meaner and tighter your life.

If someone you care about is going through a very destructive phase and no matter what you have done to try to help them all your efforts have been frustrated, then the only way to help them to help themselves is to tell them that you believe that eventually they will deal with their problems and overcome them. To say something like:

> *I know you are having a really tough time but you*
> *need to know that I have total belief that you will*
> *find a way through it. If you need me, I'm here, but*
> *I trust in your ability to solve these problems in your*
> *own way in your own time.*

That is the kind of praise that sustains us all.

On a more everyday level, when you are dealing with a frustrating or a potentially explosive situation, do not indulge yourself in an expression of rage or personal abuse, but attempt to defuse the situation by asking that person to help you. For example, if you arrive at the airport luggage department and the scales show that you are overweight and the person behind the counter is doing a good imitation of a Nazi general, attack or any form of negative comment is totally counterproductive. Your relationship, however brief, with this person is the only thing that can save you.

Once when I was returning to Australia from several years overseas I had too much hand luggage. I explained to the official, who was adamant that I simply had to discard one of my bags, that the reason I was carrying an extra bag was that I had bought some precious pottery for my mother and my aunts, and did not want to risk breaking it as I had already carried it halfway around the world on my travels. 'Please, could you help me,' I pleaded. One of the officials took the bag and said, 'Leave it with me'. I had no choice but to trust him. I went through customs, boarded the plane and was sitting anxiously belted in my seat when down the aisle carrying my extra hand luggage came the Nazi. 'Put this in a safe place could you madam,' he said, still without cracking a smile.

To genuinely state your case and ask for help, particularly from someone who has been particularly unpleasant, is to make yourself vulnerable to rejection or even abuse. But what the hell, that is exactly what you would have received if you had attacked them. At least this way you have a chance of winning some ground or at least achieving a compromise.

I had a very big conference in Ballarat and we couldn't quite fit into the room we were meant to be in. We needed to put the registration desk in the foyer. I should have got hold of the manager in the first place and asked him if he minded. Anyway, we got it all set up and along came the manager, and he went straight into enemy mode. He was hysterical: 'How dare you do that! You've hired this room, and you didn't even bother to ask me. I will have the police down here! What happens if one of the people in this hotel trips over your desk? I'm going to have liability cases. You've got five minutes to move it all, and that's that.' He turned his back on me, and stormed off. His shoulders were hunched up, and I could hear all my people muttering. I just went into daughter mode — he was my father and he had misunderstood me. I immediately said, 'Please don't leave me, you're absolutely right. I'm so sorry. Don't go away. I'm sure you'll come up with a much better idea. Please help me.' I said this at the top of my voice across the foyer. He stopped in his tracks. He dropped his shoulders, and turned and looked at me, and I said, 'Please, I'm so sorry. You're 100 per cent correct. I'm sure you'll come up with a much better idea ...', etc. I said all this with real compassion and understanding for what I had done, and I accepted total responsibility. He came back. Sure enough, after some dialogue, he realised we hadn't acted with an intent to cause him harm. We were allowed to leave the registration desk where it was, and it wasn't a problem for the hotel or the guests. Now, if I had said, 'What a pig, what a bureaucratic twerp', we would have had to move, and quickly.

FABIAN DATTNER *Tall Poppies Too*

Fear of rejection is usually a self-fulfilling prophecy in terms of personal relationships. Sometimes people are so life-worn and bruised from past rejections that they close off any possibility of a relationship before it even has a chance. Sometimes people are just genuinely shy. Most of us experience some form of shyness or fear of being overwhelmed at some stage in our lives, most often during adolescence.

How often have you witnessed a parent saying to an adolescent, 'For God's sake, say something'. What is often taken for sulkiness or arrogance is often a genuine fear of saying the wrong thing and looking like a total klutz or nerd. In these situations the solution is to simply teach the adolescent or the adult to ask the other person a question. And then to listen to the answer and ask a follow-up question. No matter how dreary the occasion, you can usually strike up some kind of relationship with someone if you take this approach. Successful public figures are usually very good listeners. Dame Roma Mitchell, the first woman Queen's Counsel and Supreme Court Judge in Australia, told me in *The Matriarchs* that although she never married, had always lived alone, she had never been lonely and didn't ever expect to be.

> *I don't think anybody really need be lonely. There's always somebody to be interested in. It's only people who are very self-centred who get lonely. I've always had lots of friends, the young as well as my generation.*

Margaret Whitlam, former First Lady of Australia admitted to me that as a young woman she had been shy.

> *My mother would get so cross with me. I used to think I don't know any of these people. It was awful. Now it doesn't worry me at all. She jollied me out of it by saying 'Just stand there by the door, look around, and if you know anybody go up to them and if you don't know anybody then ask a question and find out who they are'. She was right. Now I'm not averse to going to the theatre, opera, concerts alone if at the last moment whoever I was going with can't go. I usually meet someone I know. It's terrific.*
>
> The Matriarchs

She had her own television interview program called *With Margaret Whitlam.*

*Television is just being interested in people, wanting
to know about them and wanting the world to
know more about them.*

The Matriarchs

As a prime minister's wife she just saw the role as 'being human towards other humans and not treating them badly. Those people who are worthwhile make you feel so good anyway. The Queen (of Britain) makes you feel totally comfortable. There's no reason in the world to feel apprehensive of an audience with her'.

Betty Pugh, printer, mystic, eccentric and 'Queen Mother' to a huge family of internationally successful painters and potters missed her eightieth birthday by only a few days. Her granddaughter said of her:

*She was valued for her wisdom and her way of
listening. She spent many hours with friends, helping
them find solutions to their problems through her
positive thinking and allowing them to feel good
about themselves. She was a giver and gave
untiringly.*

Listening to someone else's story is a form of recognition, a form of praise and of affirmation. The skill of listening is greatly undervalued.

The popularity of talk-back radio is not just about people being given the democratic right to speak on the radio, it's also about being listened to. So often in our eagerness to express an opinion we have forgotten not only the importance but the art of listening. When I was presenting a morning program in Sydney, so often people rang to thank me, not for talking to them, but for listening to them.

One of the saddest legacies of the late twentieth century is the increasing number of lonely people. It's not just that we live in big cities and have lost a sense of community and the responsibility that comes with being part of a group or a tribe, it's more importantly that we have become so obsessed with our own individual needs that we have forgotten this basic principle: the energy you give out is the energy you get back. Loneliness is a form of self-absorption. It is ironic that in this era of increasing avenues for communication because of the technological revolution — voice mail, email, faxes etc. — the number of truly isolated, lonely people is increasing.

Praise or recognition in all its forms will break down or transcend the barriers of class, race, caste, religion and particularly gender.

I don't agree that men and women are from different planets like Mars or Venus. I think that we are all imperfect earthlings who have allowed our differences, genetic, physiological and sociological, to drive us apart. Men certainly have more public power than women and that imbalance and inequality is being addressed on a daily basis. It is this imbalance in power, opportunity and equality that causes so much hostility and conflict between the sexes, not the fact that they come from different planets. Discrimination on the basis of sex, race or class is easily internalised and in order to throw off its crippling effects we have to learn to be bold. Bold enough to believe in ourselves and our talents regardless of hierarchical, institutional or structural inhibitors.

AS A PRIME MINISTER'S WIFE SHE JUST SAW THE ROLE AS 'BEING HUMAN TOWARDS OTHER HUMANS AND NOT TREATING THEM BADLY. THOSE PEOPLE WHO ARE WORTHWHILE MAKE YOU FEEL SO GOOD ANYWAY.

One of the greatest legacies of the women's movement that has swept the world in the latter part of this century is that women learned the courage to speak out and to act on the aspects of their lives with which they were unhappy. They built on the work and the boldness of the early feminists, the suffragettes and the suffragists at the beginning of the century, and took their lives into their own hands.

I was fortunate to be born in the State of South Australia which had not only been among the first states in the world to grant women the right to vote, it was also, incredibly, the first state in the world to pass legislation that allowed women to stand for parliament. And it was my State that was the first to pass the Sex Discrimination Act in the 1970s. As the women's movement seeded its ideas through the many books that validated it, women all over the world suddenly knew they were not alone. And our lives were never the same again.

The rest, as they say, is history. Partly as a backlash against this revolutionary movement and partly as a result of men's failure to adapt to the changes spawned by the new feminism, a men's movement has also emerged. Men are still in positions of power and some are still saying that feminism has got it all wrong. The reality is that women are gradually working their way into sharing those powerful positions, and the men who accept that any community needs to use the talents of all its members will be the ones who will not be left behind bitter and confused. In the late 1980s a book by Robert Bly, titled *Iron John*, urged men to undertake their own inner journey of discovery. Now it was men all over the world who read the book and who suddenly felt less alone. They recognised it as part of their own story.

Steve Biddulph was one of these men and he wrote a book called *Manhood* — part manual, part self-discovery. He said, ' I wanted to have the second forty years of my life on a different footing to my first forty'. His next book *Raising Boys* he described as 'collecting the folklore of parenting and passing it on'. Even though the suicide rates of young men are rising, he is optimistic about boys and says parents, but especially fathers, should keep on trying and there is a growing movement among younger men to spend more time with their children and to take more responsibility for parenthood than their fathers did.

Biddulph says, 'If as a man you invest in your kids, put in the time and effort, it will happen. It invites the magic in. Love has a way of settling on those who are willing to just hang out together. If you at least have a go, it counts'.

There is a growing awareness that our energy in the so-called gender debate is far better directed at acknowledging and coming to terms with the similarities between the sexes, rather than emphasising the differences. Men are from Earth and so are women.

For example, none of us has to become like the French in order to appreciate what are their best qualities. Similarly women do not have to become token men in order to attain power or to appreciate the best attributes that men bring to positions of leadership.

Men and women need to be trained in communicating with each other, honestly and openly. Giving praise is the beginning. They need to be able to express their differences and celebrate their diversity. They do not have to merge into one genderless conglomerate. The main task of this book is to help people overcome their fears and develop their courage, their boldness. It is widely acknowledged that the average person develops only 10 per cent of their potential talents because they allow other factors to hold them back.

One of the overriding problems with many people's lives today, whether they are living alone or with other people, is that they are lonely. Lonely people are the last ones ever to acknowledge their sense of isolation. Instead they develop all kinds of masks and usually compensate by over-indulging in food, alcohol or drugs, or all of these. Others just lead quiet lives of desperation. Loneliness unfortunately breeds self-absorption and self-centredness. Often people are so afraid of loneliness that they will put up with any form of abuse rather than face rejection.

The secret of solving loneliness is simple. You force yourself to stop thinking about yourself and you make yourself show some interest in other people — it doesn't matter whether they are neighbours, colleagues, former friends or school mates. The mistake that lonely people often make is in believing that somehow they have to get people interested in them.

'I couldn't possibly be his or her friend. Why would they be interested in me?'

They're not, at first. All you have to do is show some genuine interest in and concern about their lives.

If you have become so encased in your own capsule of loneliness that it is genuinely hard to feel any interest in someone else, then fake it. Most people are so involved in themselves that they wouldn't notice at first. You have to break the habit of self-centredness in order to form the new habit of friendship. You have to consciously make time to do things for or with others. A phone call, an email, a fax which shows that you are thinking about the other person and interested in their lives will make all the difference.

These are all simple, everyday things but we have forgotten them. Our excuse? Usually we say that we are too busy. Busy is an overused word that should be banned from our vocabulary. Of course we all know that we make time in any schedule for things or people that we care about. The most successful business, professional and political leaders always make time for other people. Once they stopped working at their personal relationships they began to lose it. Take Howard Hughes for example. Or Elvis. Or Nixon. Or the British Royal Family. Or you, perhaps.

8

CONFLICT: SOLVE WITH PRAISE

* Envy
* Anger
* Repression
* Control
* Circuit-breaking

How much time do you waste in conflict, big and small, with other people? That's the trouble with other people, isn't it? They don't always agree with you or see things from your point of view. Sometimes the conflict is within your own head, nagging away there like a toothache, disrupting your concentration and your sense of wellbeing.

The reality is that it's a rare day that you do not have to deal with some form of conflict. Most of us don't handle it too well. No matter how much experience you have with conflict you don't necessarily learn from it. Usually you revert back to old patterns, most of which are learned in childhood. I find that I either walk away from it like my father or I'm in it up to my eye-balls like my aunts or, like my mother, I brood over it and internalise it. None of these approaches works. Believe me.

I have read endless books on how to resolve conflict and achieve a win-win solution and still find it hard not to view such 'win-win' results as wishy-washy compromises. My most annoying stumbling blocks are with petty officials like parking inspectors. In fact anything to do with cars or parking is a minefield of conflict. How do you react when someone in another car cuts you off or cuts in on you?

Despite the fact that many men, especially young men, drive as if on permanent Viagra, it is the young women, sassy and independent, thanks to the freedom and independence that tired old tarts like myself fought for, that are among the rudest and the most aggravating drivers on the road. They steal parking spaces with no conscience, they give you the rude finger sign if you even look as if you are hesitating, they toot their horns at the slightest provocation and dare you to take them on.

Often I have come close to a re-enactment of that famous parking scene in the film *Fried Green Tomatoes* where the middle-aged Cathy Bates character, having been rudely cheated out of a parking space by two young women, decides to ram her much bigger car into theirs. When they scream, her only reply is, 'I'm older and I've got more insurance'.

Whenever I'm involved in a dispute with a parking inspector I know that aggression and abuse will get me nowhere and that it would be much smarter to hold my tongue and tell them I know they have a job to do but could they please just consider some extenuating circumstances. It would be even smarter to try to find some form of praise or recognition of the toughness of their job, especially when I really want to spit in their smug face because they know they have all the power. Why, when we are at our most powerless with our backs to the wall, do we enact scenarios which only increase our powerlessness? And then we burn and brood about it all day or bore everyone to death with the re-telling of the incident. These are not trivial examples because how you deal with these minor conflicts will determine how you deal with a major one which will really count.

If you have ever been involved in renovating a house, then you will undoubtedly have come up against local officialdom in the form of a council employee who is preventing you from doing something you think is perfectly reasonable. If you engage in open conflict, you will inevitably lose because the council has the power. The last time I renovated a house I started off really well. Just as you would prepare the soil before starting a major planting, I visited the council offices, met the person who would be dealing with my architectural plans, explained to them what I was trying to achieve. I even invited them to visit and have a look for themselves. Everything went smoothly for months until the last few days when time was running out and the builder told me the inspector had told him not to proceed with the garage. Having had to resolve all the usual traumas with both the architect and the builder, I was at my wit's end, especially when the inspector's demands would have made the security doors on the garage ineffectual. When I heard my voice rising and felt my tongue sharpening to a razor's edge, I said, 'I will get someone else to negotiate this with you', as I knew I was about to blow it. My friend took over and calmly negotiated an early concession on one point with the inspector which made him feel justified in his decision and his compromise was that the work was finally completed.

When all else fails and you know you have backed yourself into a corner, be wise enough to call in a third person and ask for help, and whether the conflict is between you and a stranger, a work colleague, a family member, friend or lover, the path to resolution is always the same.

> *I also think it is important for people to control their emotions at the time when something goes wrong or is particularly challenging. If you do, you will think far more creatively. You must assume everyone's a friend or a relative when dealing with adversity, because friends and relatives will always help above and beyond the call of duty. Never create a 'them*

versus us' mentality. If you can, get all the key
players into one room at one time, with compassion
and no enmity, and quietly present your case. I
guarantee that nine times out of ten you will come
out better than you would have had you not done
that. People tend to use the telephone or speak to
only one of four people at a time when they should
have had all four in one room at the same time.
Turning possible enemies into real friends is a
wonderful skill to acquire.

FABIAN DATTNER *Tall Poppies Too*

Every day of your life you will experience some form of conflict, major or minor. Even if you try to avoid it or ignore it, one of its friends or relatives will seek you out. Conflict is always about power, who has it, who wants it and who is prepared to fight for it. Every relationship you have involves power, even your relationship with yourself.

The first rule is to face up to conflict in the knowledge that you can deal with it. In fact the ultimate goal is to instil in yourself a genuine belief that there is no kind of conflict or situation that you can't ultimately deal with well. Life sometimes throws us some very nasty surprises but no matter what they are you must confront them head-on. Avoidance of conflict is only delaying the inevitable. If you sense that some kind of conflict or power struggle is brewing between you and another person, don't wait for it to burst its skin like a boil and spew forth its poison or to fester beneath the surface infecting other aspects of your life.

Face it by saying, 'I have noticed that ... do we have a problem? If so, let's discuss it'. If you are confronted with denial which is often the first reaction — 'Problem? No. Certainly not. Whatever gave you that impression?' — then say, 'Fine, but if after thinking about it you realise that something is not quite right please don't hesitate to talk to me'. If the other person has been waiting for you to broach the topic, as is often the case, then don't hesitate to emphasise your willingness to resolve it. Unresolved conflict is the cause of all breakdowns in relationships, personal and professional.

Just to signal your willingness to sit down with someone, to take the time to listen to them and to do what you can to resolve the conflict amicably, is a form of praise. It recognises the validity of the other person and their feelings.

> *Out of every hundred people that you meet, one*
> *might be impossible to work with. I'm not hurt by it*
> *but I feel sorry for them. I simply say, 'There's no*
> *place here for you, find somewhere else, because*
> *you're hurting yourself and you're hurting us'. I*
> *don't like arguments, and I don't like people*
> *complaining. If I have people bitching or sniggering*
> *behind one another I'll say, 'If you've got a*
> *problem, bring it out in the open'.*
>
> FABIAN DATTNER *Tall Poppies Too*

To hit a brick wall of denial when you first broach the subject can often result in anger, which is the least useful emotion when resolving conflict. Recognise it as the other person's failure to confront the truth and wait for another time when you have an example or an incident that you can use as a starting point. You can't force someone to deal with conflict unless they are ready. Any attempt to force the issue will put you further behind in your attempts at resolution. Anger will render you powerless and this sense of powerlessness will only exacerbate the conflict.

However, no-one is ever totally powerless. You first have to believe that you have power, regardless of the situation; that belief will be communicated to the other person. Power always starts with you. Recognise the power that you have. Do not start from the position of whining, powerless victim. If you do find yourself in conflict with someone in a position of authority over you, then attack is never the best form of defence. This is a lesson that has been a hard one for me to learn. Having spent a large part of my life working inside large bureaucratic structures, like a university or the Australian Broadcasting Commission, I found I was perpetually involved in clashes of egos, substance and style. Envy also is often a hidden player. Try to work out what is the real cause of the conflict.

When I published my first book, *Tall Poppies,* it became an immediate best-seller. I expected foolishly that my colleagues and, more importantly, my supervisors in the university would be pleased for me and for the reflected success on the institution. Instead, I found not only stony silence on the topic but snide remarks about becoming rich on the book's royalties. And with each successive and successful book, a slow realisation dawned on me that far from being praised for my success in the outside world, I was being punished for it inside the academic world. Those with power, and I must admit they were often women who would have described themselves as feminists, seemed determined to ensure that none of my published work would ever count as evidence for academic recognition or promotion. This was truly the politics of envy and I had no way of dealing with it other than to ignore it. Again success was viewed as a pie and if one person had a slice then it was assumed that there was less for everyone else. All my attempts to argue that my public success was a bridge between the university and the community fell on deaf ears. The unspoken view was that I had received more than my fair share of recognition and praise. My public profile for an academic was already too high.

It took me a long time to come to terms with the fact that my academic colleagues would never give me any recognition for my work, even though my teaching and my writing in the field of communications were so closely intertwined.

C. S. Lewis, the English writer, experienced similar lack of promotion at Oxford University because he had achieved public success in his BBC broadcasts. Public praise, whatever form it takes, will often bring you in conflict with other people. Far too often we allow other people's envy to eat away at our confidence, which is why it is such a destructive emotion both for those who are envious and for those who are the object of envy. In order to minimise the whiplash effect of public success I have noticed that some people down-play all attempts at praise. For example, when Geoffrey Rush won an Oscar for best actor in the film *Shine* I noticed that he went out of his way to prove that it really was no big deal and that fame would not change him. After the initial burst of world-wide publicity he did not splash his face across every newspaper and magazine in endless interviews and when he did make public utterances they were always suitably self-effacing. How sad that he couldn't just let it all go and be able to luxuriate in what he had achieved by giving himself some praise for all his hard work over the years.

The actor Emma Thompson believes that our reaction to success and praise is culturally based and believes that America loves you when you are successful, ignores you when you are a failure, whereas in Britain, and I would add Australia, the opposite is true. When you experience some kind of public flop in Britain or Australia, all your mates rally around. The most successful Australian playwright, David Williamson, openly admits that he never experienced real vitriol until he became publicly successful in Australia.

So often when we find ourselves in conflict with other people, hidden envy is at the base of it. Rarely is anyone openly envious and yet to speak your envy is to release it. To be able to say to someone, 'I really envy your success, or your relationship, or your life' stops the envy eating away at you, paralysing you. Having said it, released it, you are free to go on and say 'perhaps you could give me some advice or help in my own attempts'.

Most successful people when confronted with such honesty will be pleased to give you the benefit of their experience. To ask for help or advice is a form of praise; if for some reason the request is rebutted or ignored then you have lost nothing in the asking and perhaps realised that this person is not worthy of your envy.

If having tried all methods to avoid conflict with someone who refuses to acknowledge that it is their envy that is causing conflict with you, then you have to let go and move on.

When I finally stopped banging my head against the promotional brick wall at the university I had two choices. One was to give up writing books and spend my time on academic papers and committee work, the other was to expand my work in writing and communication with the aim of leaving the university and starting an alternative career where my work would be appreciated. I chose the latter path and never looked back. Disappointed though I was with my university colleagues, there was no point in continuing the conflict, especially when the winds of economic rationalism were beginning to sweep through the campus. Courses like mine in creative writing, which meant classes no larger than twenty students, were targeted because of the economic formulas being applied. You have to express it and then let the anger go, no matter how justified you feel you are.

> IF YOU CAN MAINTAIN A SENSE OF BELIEF IN YOUR OWN TALENTS, YOU ALWAYS HAVE CHOICES. SO OFTEN WE INTERNALISE OTHER PEOPLE'S CRITICISMS AND ALLOW THEM TO CONTROL OUR LIVES.

In 1994, apart from my frustrations at work, I found myself in conflict with the Board of Governors of the Adelaide Festival of Arts and the senior managers of ABC Television. It was a ripper of a year. In every situation I was powerless to effect change because those with whom I was disagreeing had all the power. There are some battles that you can never win but what you can negotiate with yourself is how you deal with those facts. If you can maintain a sense of belief in your own talents, you always have choices. So often we internalise other people's criticisms and allow them to control our lives. Even the great English novelist Thomas Hardy gave up writing because of criticism of his work.

One of Eleanor Roosevelt's famous sayings is that 'no-one can make you feel inferior without your consent'. In other words when you allow other people's words or actions with whom you are in conflict to destroy your confidence you must know that you are colluding in this. You can become a collaborator in your own downfall. Don't get morose; move on. So many of us carry around long-held resentments which are really just repressed anger. Anger then manifests itself as a form of depression.

So how did I deal with this avalanche of criticism that seemed determined to swamp me in 1994? With Eleanor Roosevelt's words as my mantra (I always had them pinned up on a poster in my academic office for me as well as the students) I cast back in my mind for some words of praise that I had received. And they were there. So often when we get criticism and praise, all we can remember is the criticism. Every writer will tell you that despite many good reviews they always remember, in detail, the bad ones.

In March of that year I had been the Chair of the International Writers' Festival at the Adelaide Festival of Arts and two of the visiting writers were Marilyn French, author of the best-selling classic *The Women's Room* and Deirdre Bair, the award-winning biographer of Simone de Beauvoir, the greatest woman writer and catalyst of our time, whom she had been fortunate enough to meet and get to know. At the end of the Writers' Festival, which had been acclaimed as a great success, I found myself in conflict with the Board of Governors who subsequently sacked me and my entire committee. I then thought back to an idea that I had briefly discussed with Deirdre Bair about a book based on interviews with the most influential women writers still alive, those whose books had really changed the world. I rang her in New York and she was not only encouraging but offered to ring her extensive network of contacts in order to help me. There is no greater praise or recognition than an offer of help. I knew that one of the women I would need in such a book was Marilyn French. Buoyed up by her remark that my interview with her for my television program *Susan Mitchell: In Conversation* was the best she had ever done, I rang her to ask if, despite the fact that she was still waging a huge battle of recovery from cancer, she would agree to take the time to be in this book. 'Well,' she said after a long pause, 'I wouldn't normally agree but I will do it. For you'. I could have whooped with joy. All I needed to get me started on what I knew would be my most exciting and challenging book to date was this one act of kindness and generosity. By June of the next year I was in New York with ten days scheduled to interview the ten most influential writers of the world. I was to become the narrator of their lives and work.

The irony is that if the Board of Governors had not dispensed with my services I would never have thought of writing such a book because I would have been too preoccupied with planning the next Writers' Festival. It wasn't that I had not raged publicly and wept privately at their decision, I had simply in the end refused to let it crush me. In the words of the psychologists, I had turned a negative into a positive. But before I hit the streets of New York in June 1995 I had a book to write on women and politics in Australia. Prior to beginning that I had lost another battle which I and my team had been waging for the past year with the senior management of ABC Television.

As time would have it, I began work on the book, *The Scent of Power,* on the same day that my last program went to air. Clutching the farewell flowers in a taxi on my way to the airport, I was still in the grip of the emotional roller coaster that inevitably accompanies this kind of conflict and turmoil. How much of this year's battles had I brought upon myself? Was it partly because I was over-opinionated, overweight and over forty? These were the difficult years for all women and I knew I was thought to be 'uppity'. Certainly 'uppity' in the eyes of those patriarchs on the Board of Governors and those bureaucrats in the ABC who were all most displeased with the fact that I had fought such a hard and public battle. I was still stinging from the male fist of power. As I said in my first chapter of *The Scent of Power*:

> *Perhaps I should have done what they told me.*
> *Crawled into a corner, licked my wounds and shut*
> *my mouth. And kept it shut, despite the media's*
> *questions, in the faint hope that sometime in the*
> *future those same men might offer me a few crumbs*

from the high table.
I didn't believe them, I still don't believe them. So
why did I take on a public fight I knew I couldn't
win? Because it's not in my nature to walk away
from injustice. One of my high school reports had
stated, 'Susan becomes very angry over real or
imagined injustices'. That really made me angry.
Even in the 1960s I knew that I had not imagined
the injustices inherent in the ways in which girls at
the school were treated compared to boys. Now, of
course, they have programs to counteract inequality
in schools. Was I still fighting that same battle? I
certainly felt that same anger, that same sense of
powerlessness.
And yet here I was in a taxi on my way to the
airport to catch a plane to Canberra, to write a book
on women in Federal Parliament. It was a rerun of
all my old high school experiences. Was I crazy?
Wouldn't it be easier just to throw myself out of this
moving car? Canberra, the house on the hill, the last
male bastion, the seat of power. Or was it?
It was ironic that my final television interview had
been with Frederick Forsyth, who was in Adelaide
to promote his latest book, The Fist of God. *Like*
all his other books it was a macho, fast-moving saga
of men involved in war, politics and espionage. No
major parts for women. The author himself was just
like one of his heroes: cool, urbane, English, self-
composed, charming.
'Who really has the power in this world?' I had
asked him. 'Is it governments, the CIA, the
multinationals, the media barons?'
His reply: 'Bureaucrats'.
Surprised though I was at his certainty, I did not
demur. I was still nursing those wounds from the
male ABC bureaucrats who had taken no notice of

petitions from both sides of politics, no notice of the
hundreds of letters from viewers, no notice of my
reasoned arguments — but that's another story, best
told in fiction. Like many politicians, particularly
female politicians, my departure from television was
more memorable than my arrival. Particularly as
the timing of that departure was not of my choosing.
Television is a lot like politics, both tough games
that take no prisoners. Usually, just when you start
to think you've mastered the skills, you're given the
push. Departures in both television and politics are
always hard because they are so public.
'That's all behind you now. Let it go. Move on,' I said
to myself as the taxi pulled up in front of Departures.

For the rest of that year I documented and analysed the lives and the power struggles of all the women who had been or were major participants in the game of politics as it is played in Australia. I relived all their heartaches, their disappointments, their frustrations and their victories. And by the end of the book I had learnt a great deal about conflict and about power. I did not get my television program back nor my chairmanship of the Writers' Festival committee. This is real life, not Hollywood. And I wasn't sure that I had entirely mastered the skills of 'win-win' negotiation or conflict resolution but I had learnt to recognise envy in other people as something I could not fight, I had learnt how to turn my anger into positive action and not let it cement itself into a solid block of resentment. And more importantly, I had learnt to use other people's praise as a catalyst for moving on to positive action. The power of praise is that it can transport you or catapult you into a new place. All of the praise you have ever received is deposited in your memory bank; so too is all the criticism. You always have a choice. Do you withdraw the praise or the criticism and put it in your wallet? Praise will make you feel powerful; criticism powerless. But you can't keep making withdrawals without keeping up the deposits. It's important that you not only make deposits of praise in other people's accounts but also in your own.

Herb Cohen, who wrote a best-selling book called *You Can Negotiate Anything,* describes winning as 'managing the outcome by seeing your reality true and clear and being able to react with the appropriate strategy. Winning means fulfilling your needs while being consistent with your beliefs and values'.

He emphasised the fact that sometimes even though you win the conflict you make a life-time enemy. This is usually called winning the battle and losing the war. Most of us know that we will lose arguments or relationships or jobs but the thing we hate to lose most is 'face'. We hate to be humiliated, belittled, made to feel 'small' in front of other people. We also hate people who do that to others.

A friend of mine, who was once a Commissioner on the Public Service Board and therefore had to make judgements at disciplinary hearings, recounted an incident to me where a public servant who had an impeccable record of over thirty years had made a false claim for expenses involving less than $100. The prosecuting lawyer who was intent on demonstrating her talents, however, humiliated him in front of the tribunal. The man received an extremely light punishment because the Commissioner considered that the public indignity which the accused had been forced to undergo was far more punishment than anything they could administer.

Herb Cohen points out that 'even when you are right, shun all opportunities to humiliate people — at least in public. Remember this, not only for them, but for yourself as well'. The person who boasts that they have won and made their opponent 'look like a fool' is themselves a fool. Even if you have every reason to dislike or even loathe the person with whom you are in conflict, you must resist the urge to humiliate them or decimate them in front of another person. In the short term it may be very gratifying and make for a very good story to tell your mates but ultimately it is self-indulgent and counterproductive. Having always fancied myself as an aficionado of the verbal stoush, this has been a hard lesson for me to learn. I confess that, at times, I find it hard to resist having the last word.

But as the Joey Brown character in *Some Like It Hot* said to the Jack Lemmon character who told him that he couldn't possibly marry him because he was a man, 'So what. Nobody's perfect'.

The conflict that really eats at your heart and soul is of course the conflict you experience with your family, your lovers and your friends. All of these people know your vulnerabilities, just as you know theirs. It is so easy for you to have conflict with those people you care deeply about. All families are strange and dysfunctional, to varying degrees. But we always think that other people's families are happier, more stable, less destructive than ours. Sometimes of course they are. But most often when you really get to know what really happens on the inside of what you imagine to be a version of *The Brady Bunch* you end up thinking, 'They are all crazier and more dysfunctional than my lot'.

A friend of mine who was a single parent was having a great deal of trouble with her fourteen-year-old daughter who said that she hated the family she had and wanted to move into the large happy family who owned the paper round that she worked at after school. She even spoke to the mother of this family, told her how unhappy she was and wondered if they had room for an adopted daughter. This woman rang my friend, who was feeling greatly distressed and humiliated by her daughter. I convinced my friend to let her daughter move in with these people on a trial basis in the full knowledge that if she didn't like it, she could come home. Three weeks later she was back in her own room, telling her mother that they were all 'so bland and boring and they actually ate white, sliced bread'.

How often when you are complaining about the problems you are having with a member of your family do you think about what you would say if you had to praise that person? Imagine that you have to find three things about the problem family member that are praiseworthy. Once you have managed to dredge up one or two, try to weave them into a conversation either with the 'problem' person or someone in the family you know will repeat what you have said to them. You will be amazed how this one gift of praise will change the dynamic of your relationship.

Think about how hard it is to get really angry with someone you have been told thinks that you are either very smart or very sexy or even both. Always in the back of your mind when you meet that person is the knowledge that they secretly hold these praiseworthy opinions of you. Most families are hotbeds of conflict but usually when the chips are down, their conflicts are forgotten. If they aren't, then it's probably therapy time. When friends or lovers betray you or let you down or hurt you and you feel that there is no point in continuing the relationship, the end usually involves some kind of conflict.

It's healthy to express your hurt and then to listen to the other person's reaction, which is usually defensive. Sometimes it's very good to shout and scream and let it all out but when you have said it all, don't delude yourself that it is over. Catharsis is not closure. If you really do want to end the relationship in a way that won't lodge in your throat like a bitter pill that you can't seem to swallow, then try acknowledging the qualities that you liked in the person and recognise that you did share some good times together. Acknowledge this either face to face or if that is too hard, by writing a personal note.

If, however, you are the one who is being accused of the hurt or the betrayal, then there is no point in trying to defend yourself. Simply write a letter in which you say that you are sorry that this person feels this way, that you acknowledge their feelings, that you have valued them and what you have shared. To recognise the fact that you have hurt someone is a validation of their feelings and validation is a form of praise. And giving praise to those you have hurt or been hurt by is a means of resolving the conflict in a way that will lead to healing.

You can't make someone love you if they don't, you can't make someone fall back in love with you if they can't, all you can do is recognise the fact that they did love you and that you had the best of it. Only then can you move on. To go on and on, berating them, punishing them, despising them is a way of not letting go.

We all know we get back what we give out and to give pain to someone else is also to give it to ourselves. To give recognition that you once shared something valuable with that person, and perhaps you have even had children as a result of that sharing, is to focus on the fact that you can now move on to something better. Let those old green garbage bags of anger, depression and resentments go off in the rubbish where they belong. If a piece of fruit is bruised, you don't keep the bruised bit and throw away the rest. You enjoy the bit that is still good.

Besides, how can you expect someone new to want to get to know you when you are 'on the nose' with all that stinking old garbage you insist on carrying around with you?

9
COMMUNICATE: WITH PRAISE

* Listening
* Reassurance
* Honesty
* Intimacy
* Saying 'Thank you'

Never before in the history of civilisation, have human beings had more means of communicating with each other. Letters, mobile telephones, faxes, Internet, email. And yet so often we fail to connect. We fail to say what it is we really want to say, we constantly get the wrong kind of message, the words slip and slide.

The Internet is daily creating a global village because it allows us to connect with other human beings and feel less alone. In this connection or lack of it, lies our joy or our despair. With so many tools at our fingertips, why can't we do it better?

How to connect? It's quite simple. Try praise but praise in its many forms. Try listening, for example. Really listening to what someone is saying is a very high form of praise. Think about how you feel when you are talking and you know the other person is not listening — their eyes are glazed or darting around the room. They are constantly looking, not at you but somewhere over your right shoulder. They are nodding but their body is turned away from you. We have all experienced this and we have all done it to someone else, even though we know it is very belittling. It makes the talker feel small. Lesser somehow.

Now think about how you feel when the person to whom you are talking makes eye contact, gives you their total and undivided attention, listens to what you are saying because they ask questions that follow on. This is praise indeed. You feel that what you are saying is interesting, important. You feel interesting and 'big'. Expanded.

The skills of listening are basic to all communication. How often did you hear that the late Princess Diana's real talent was that when she talked with someone, she made them feel as if they were the only person in the world. We all crave that sense, that we are important, that we count. The cruel irony of Princess Diana was that only in death did she receive the kind of recognition and praise that she had craved her entire life.

The skills of listening are active skills. Start with the person's name. How often do you actively practise remembering the names of people you are introduced to? We all know how impressed we are when someone we have only been introduced to once remembers our name and we are positively glowing when they remember what we were talking about.

The reason that we envy the celebrity is that no-one forgets their name and their every word is hung upon. Fame is having other people recognise your name and who you are. Of course some people crave that recognition so much they are prepared to kill in order to receive it.

Human beings in the late twentieth century are egocentric and most good salesmen know this, so they make a point of remembering the names of good customers, the names of their families, their likes and dislikes. It's amazing how well we respond to a salesperson who remembers our name. The average person loves to hear the sound of their own name or to see it printed. Why else do companies publicly list their sponsors, why do festivals sell naming rights, why do rich people attempt to get their names recorded in as many places as possible, why do politicians open buildings and unveil plaques?

Dale Carnegie believed that 'the ability to remember names is almost as important in business and social contacts as it is in politics'. He revealed that Napoleon the Third, Emperor of France, employed this technique. If you don't hear the person's name, say 'I'm sorry, I didn't get the name clearly'. Then if it was an unusual name he said, 'How is it spelt?' During the conversation he took the trouble to repeat the name several times and tried to associate it with the person's features, expression and general appearance.

I know as a lecturer that the faster I remembered the names of my students the better my communication with them. I would usually ask them to introduce themselves to the class and tell us a story about their childhood. The next week when we all came together I would ask one student to introduce another and re-tell what he had said. This also impressed upon them the value of listening, really listening.

Remembering what someone has said is a form of praise. It is a recognition that what you have said really counts. As an interviewer, the skills of listening are essential. So often you see someone conducting an interview, going from one question to another, without listening to the answers. Hundreds of people have written to me over the years to ask me firstly how to interview someone and secondly how I managed to get people to reveal so much about themselves. I tell them the secret. Listen to what they tell you, put yourself in their shoes, see the world through their eyes and you will become totally absorbed in what they are saying. Once a person senses that you are genuinely interested in them and on the same wavelength, it's amazing what they will tell you.

Not that communication is a one-way process. If you ask questions you also have to be prepared to give something of yourself if you are asked. Although, once people get involved in talking about themselves, you can't stop most of them. But once you stop listening attentively and they sense that your interest is waning, they will either stop or revert to more formal conversation. Often when friends ring or visit in order to ask you for help or advice, all they want is for you to be a good listener. They work through what is troubling them and then thank you for your help when in reality you've probably said very little.

The best method for dealing with a disgruntled or irritated colleague, friend or customer is to listen to them and let them talk without interrupting. Psychologists use this simple technique of letting the person vent their feelings in a totally haphazard way, usually illogically and with no real order. Then they focus on the main emotion and say, 'So you are feeling angry/hurt/anxious because ...' And the person then focuses on the real reason for their outburst having had their version listened to without any interruptions or comments.

If listening is such a powerful positive skill in our lives and in communication, then why are most of us so bad at it? Hugh Mackay, in his book *The Good Listener*, summarises his findings by emphasising that often people don't listen to us because we don't listen to them. They do listen when they know that what we say shows an understanding of them. They do listen when we have taken their feelings into account and don't expect too much agreement at once. They do listen when they sense we are in touch with ourselves — in other words do we listen to ourselves?

Our relationship with ourselves is again an important and often neglected aspect of communication. Mackay says, 'If our willingness to listen to others will fuel their self-esteem and reassure them that they are taken seriously as persons entitled to an opinion, we need to give the same attention to ourselves'.

If you are out of touch with your own feelings you usually have low self-esteem. The question then becomes, 'If I am not interested in myself, why should anyone else be?'

The other reason he tells us that we fail to listen is that we lack the courage to do it. Real listening involves the risk of having to change our minds in response to what we hear. 'When we listen, we make ourselves vulnerable because we put ourself outside the comfort and security of our own cage.' To learn the skills of real listening is to grow as a person.

In his book *On Becoming a Person* Carl Rogers said, 'The risk of being changed is one of the most frightening prospects most of us can face'. Mackay emphasises that 'to be truly listened to is to receive a precious gift from someone who is saying, in effect, "I am prepared to put my own interests and concerns on hold; I am putting you first; I am going to entertain your ideas"'. Unfortunately many people are so starved for that kind of listening that they have to pay therapists to do it. When we are communicating with each other we are each other's therapists or listeners.

The other aspect of good listening is to be non-judgemental. As soon as we sense that what we are saying is being judged or criticised by the person who is listening then we become defensive, overreactive or else we clam up. Real communication can only happen in an atmosphere of trust. If you are unsure about whether someone is going to attack you or be critical of you, then you will always hold back. The power of good listening will not only help someone else, it will help you. As Mackay reinforces, 'The more we communicate with other people, the clearer we become about our own sense of identity. Being understood and accepted by others is one of the most reassuring and comforting of human experiences'. To feel that you are not alone, that you belong, that you are loved, is what human beings crave at the deepest level. There can be no greater form of praise.

Our relationships with each other are the bulwarks against those times when we feel most threatened and vulnerable. Communication is the basis of all personal relationships at home or at work. We are always hearing that marital or work relationships are in trouble because of a 'breakdown in communication'.

Sometimes with the best will and intentions you just cannot persuade someone to talk to you. So often men are blamed for never talking and it is assumed that women are somehow biologically better programmed for talking about their feelings.

No-one has been able to explain this scientifically, which means that a more plausible explanation is that part of a woman's role is to create harmony out of conflict, order out of chaos, and so she is trained at an early age and expected to have the ability to be sensitive to other people's feelings. Men, on the other hand, are not expected to be open and skilled at speaking about their feelings. It is not deemed 'masculine'. As a result many men are often trapped in their loneliness and fail to work out why their relationships with their wives and their children fail. They also have difficulty in communicating with other men. So-called mateship is really just a form of ritualised grunting.

There is a growing number of enlightened men who are attempting to change their behaviour. One of the areas in which they are particularly constipated and repressed is in their ability to express praise. They may praise their wives to their mates at the pub when they have had a few drinks but rarely, if ever, do they tell them face to face how much they appreciate and recognise their efforts.

Women are now demanding more out of their marriages than a good breadwinner and a nice house. They want communication, not just conversation. They want praise, not just approval. They want recognition, not just acceptance. They want intimacy, not just sex.

Often when I begin a keynote address at a conference largely composed of men, I begin by asking, 'How many of you men rang home this morning to say thank you? Thank you for doing double the work while you are away. Thank you for being such a good wife and mother'. Very few of them put up their hands. 'Why?' I ask them. 'Why is thank you such a hard word to say? Do you know how less cranky your wife would be if you took the time to praise her efforts, to show her you recognise that her role is not always an easy one? Why is that such a hard ask? Perhaps,' I say, 'you should send her some flowers with a simple note of thank you. If only you knew how powerful that would be in making your lives happier'. One of them usually responds, 'My wife would think I was having an affair if I did that'. 'And what', I ask, 'does that say about you?' That the only time you praise her, that you recognise her worth or send her a present is when you are lying or covering something up?

What does that say about communication in your marriage? What does that teach your children?'

Then I move onto the work front. 'How many of you have rung work and thanked those back at the office who are having to make up for your time here at the conference, for their extra effort?' Again, only a few put up their hands. 'Why,' I ask them, 'should people put themselves out to do extra work when no-one is going to recognise it? Why are you so mean with praise? Why are your communication skills so narrow? If you want them not to lie to you about what is really happening in your absence, why haven't you established some form of mutual trust? If you asked a question, was it accusatory? Were you critical in any way? Did you ask any personal questions about them? For example, "How's that sore knee?" Did you listen when they tried to explain something that had gone wrong? Did you interrupt? Were you judgemental? Did you notice how often you used the pronoun "I"?'

Then I ask them to hold up their mobile phones. I ask them if they have access to email. Of course they nod. So why haven't they used them as a means of praise and recognition? If most productivity is based upon the quality of communication between the managers and the workers, many of them are in trouble.

Whether the relationship is personal, political or corporate makes no difference. Whether a government is elected depends entirely upon the way in which it communicates its message to the voters. Whether a business continues to grow depends entirely upon the way in which it communicates its message to its consumers. In this era of economic rationalism, downsizing and cutbacks, the communication between managers and workers is vital. How a government treats a public servant who has given efficient and loyal service but whose area of work is being downsized will have everything to do with how that government is perceived in the community.

When we win a job everyone congratulates us, when we lose a job, even through no fault of our own, we feel as if we have failed. How you leave a job has everything to do with how you will approach your future. In this era of corporate takeovers, those who are the victims are often treated very badly. No-one takes the time to thank them for their past work, to organise some kind of farewell for them, to wish them the best for their future. The most vicious face of capitalism is the one that treats human beings as if they are dispensable, like an empty McDonald's carton, chucked into the trash once its use is over. People who are treated in that way will often repeat this behaviour if the situation is reversed. They have felt punished and will in turn punish when their opportunity comes. This results in a totally dysfunctional workforce. Everyone, whether it's the CEO or the lowest paid worker in the corporation, needs to be praised or at least recognised as a human being, not as a number to be crunched. The 'slashers and burners', the kings of 'downsizing' have not proved to be the great salvation to business that they promised. While there may be some initial economic benefits, those businesses that have been slashed to the bone have ultimately failed to grow. Banks have increased their profits to their shareholders but alienated their customers. If you cut back a plant to its roots and fail to water or feed it, new growth will not happen. It won't necessarily die but will remain a stunted stump.

Governments who treat their workers badly will pay the price. So too their corporate equivalents. Employers of all kinds, small and multinational, need a new mantra and that mantra should be 'the power of praise'.

So make a phone call, write a note, send an email or a fax and thank someone or many people for their efforts. Never underestimate the power of a simple 'thank you'.

> *Marilyn* [French] *had booked us a table at a nearby restaurant. Elegantly dressed as always, she took my arm for steadiness and we walked, arm in arm, the two blocks to dinner. At least in New York people did not come up to us and tell her she made them leave their husbands.*
> *There was an easy physical presence about her that made me feel we had taken this walk every night for*

years. She possessed the dignity of someone who
refuses to be bowed down or diminished by her illness.
Over dinner, even though she did not eat very much,
she enjoyed my pleasure in the food and we talked
about her new novel My Summer With George.
Nothing will ever stop her writing. To her it is like
breathing.
It was a warm, pleasant night and as we strolled
back to the apartment after dinner I told her how
my book never would have been started without her
initial support. She dismissed her part in it. Praise is
still not something she accepts with ease. Criticism,
it seems, is much more familiar territory.
I persisted. I thanked her for believing in me and
the book. I thanked her for what she had given me.
I knew it had not been easy to relive all the pain
that she had experienced. It had taken great
courage. And honesty.
'I'm a survivor', she said.
'No, Marilyn, you're much more than that.'

Icons, Saints and Divas

If I had to leave behind one idea that would endure — just one — it would be to communicate as crisply and powerfully as I could that the way to connect with each other, with each other's villages and cities and countries, the way to connect with each other's ideas, beliefs and hopes is through praise. Only praise.

10

WORK: CRYING OUT FOR PRAISE

* Power
* Motivation
* Identification
* Loyalty
* Leadership

Most of us spend a large part of our lives at work. Even if the nature of work is changing rapidly and most people will have several career changes in their lives or, perhaps, an endless series of part-time or contract working relationships, one aspect will never change. And that is our need to have what we do recognised. Recognised and valued.

WORKERS ARE CRYING OUT FOR PRAISE.
SO ARE MANAGERS.

In the middle of writing this chapter I watched the Golden Globe Awards and realised that acting is one profession where, if you do well, you receive acclaim. Perhaps people who choose acting or performing as a profession crave praise more than most. To stand on a stage and hear the crescendo of clapping hands or the roar of bravos and whistles must be the most exciting and empowering form of praise. And what do we say whenever we are cheered or clapped? Thank you. We say thank you. (For making me feel so warm, so appreciated, so worthy.) And that is why all award-giving ceremonies develop a predictable pattern. After the winner's name is called and they accept the prize or the award, they thank all the people who have helped them along the way. While this may be tedious in the extreme for those watching or listening, it is very important for those who have worked hard to help this person achieve success, that they are recognised by name and thanked. This is a dramatic and heightened example of how all workers should be treated.

As a teacher of many years, I suspect that the reason most people are so mean with praise is that most teachers use it so sparingly or withhold it as a form of punishment. The reason for this is that as a profession they receive so little praise. Rare indeed is the principal who regularly takes the time to praise each teacher individually, and if there are criticisms, rare that they are framed in such a way that the teacher knows the principal has their best interests at heart.

In my first year of teaching I was also completing a post-graduate course which meant that three times a week I had to leave the school immediately classes finished in order to be at university classes on time. I discovered that a fellow teacher was badmouthing me in the staffroom over what she saw to be my lack of hard work and dedication shown by my not staying behind after school. Shocked and unsure how to tackle this in my first professional employment, I confided my problem to an older teacher on the staff whom everyone respected and asked for her help and advice. 'Leave it with me and don't worry about it' was her only reply. A week later the principal called me into his office and explained that he had been told about my concern, that I was not to worry and more importantly that he wanted to assure me that he was very happy with my work. Greatly relieved, I returned to my teaching with renewed vigour and my critic was clearly told by the principal the truth of the matter and in time she became one of my supporters. Only much later did I realise that if I hadn't confronted a problem the principal would not have given me that positive feedback. None of the other new teachers were given it.

Do you ever get positive feedback from your boss? Leadership is about giving direction. How do employees know if they are doing good work or at least heading in the right direction if they are never told by their employers? The key to leadership is communication. Managers must foster a close relationship between themselves and their staff. They should keep them informed of the organisation's performance goals and whether they have been achieved. But communication is a two-way process and there must exist in the structure a means whereby staff can inform management of their concerns. Rewards should always be seen to be aligned with performance. However, rewards do not always have to be monetary or career advancement. A written or verbal word of praise, a pat on the back are also rewards for doing something well. Do you give it to those who work with or for you? How often?

Even the executive producer of the film that won the Golden Globe Awards said, 'Praise is better than money'. While not everyone would go that far, so often in tough times or when monetary rewards are not possible employers forget that praise or recognition of hard work and effort is a great motivation for the staff. Praise is needed at all levels, even for the CEO. So often I am told by CEOs of large organisations, 'Bonuses are great but if only there was a note that said we know how hard you have worked to achieve this goal and we appreciate it, rather than just an increase in your pay packet'.

How do you react when your work is praised? Sometimes workers are so unused to praise they don't know how to deal with it. A senior bureaucrat told me about a promising young woman in her department to whom she constantly gave positive feedback. After six months she asked her, 'How are things going?' The young woman replied, 'I've liked it all but the praise. It made me feel uncomfortable'. The senior manager said, 'Okay. Well I'll stop it'. Two months later the young woman came back to her and said, 'I miss the praise'. So she continued to get it, together with a well-earned promotion and increase in salary for her good work.

We know all this to be true for children but somehow with increase in age goes decrease in praise. The need, however, never changes. When a five year old does a drawing or a painting, no matter how good or bad, the good parent sticks it up on a board or the fridge. The child beams at the recognition of its effort and seeing it there is a constant reinforcement of praise. Five or fifty years of age should make no difference. We all respond to this kind of attention.

Governments all over the world have moved to a policy of individuals taking responsibility for their own lives and those of their children but they often forget to reward those who do this in their efforts to penalise those who fail to do so. Social justice is about earning as well as giving but unless earning is recognised and rewarded you will produce a culture of taking what you can get away with. Individual effort should always be rewarded but that should not be confused with neglecting or punishing those who fail to succeed. They must be given incentives to keep trying. Most people want the self-respect and public acknowledgment of making a contribution to their society, through their work, whatever it is.

Making employees feel appreciated, focusing attention on their good ideas, inviting them to extend themselves and saying, 'Thank you. We know that you are a good employee. We value you and your work', is a big factor in motivation.

> *I am a great believer in positive feedback. Praise builds people. It's one of the great tragedies that most people don't understand how powerful it is. Instead of criticism, what I say is, 'Knowing you as I know you, and knowing how clever you are, you can do better'.*
>
> *You become what you think. Your most dominant*

thought is what you become.
The work I do is a lot of fun for everyone. Perhaps
we take ourselves too seriously. I get a thrill from
watching people blossom. They blossom because they
have a little success. I lavish praise on them for this.
I think that fundamentally this is one of the biggest
things we are missing as grown-ups — praise for
doing something right.

FABIAN DATTNER *Tall Poppies Too*

All successful companies practise implementing these non-monetary rewards, both privately and publicly. You can never overdo it. In fact you should always be thinking of new ways to do it. People work for money but they will go the extra mile for recognition, praise and rewards. Good leaders never forget this. It doesn't matter what the economic cycle, the political leanings of the government, the level of the stock market, human needs remain the same. And we all crave praise. We all need to feel that our efforts are valued. One of the biggest challenges facing the corporate world in this climate of rapid economic change where companies are daily being merged or restructured, is the management of workers where layoffs are minimised and displaced people are ensured retraining.

Every time an organisation treats one of its workers as a statistic instead of as a human being, this has a ripple effect and all workers feel undervalued. When people who have worked for the organisation and given good and loyal service are given notice and management makes no effort to farewell them or thank them, loyalty is dead.

Time and again we read or hear about people who are forced to organise their own farewell parties merely in order to mark an ending of something in their life. Particularly in this period of 'economic rationalism', it is even more important that workers who, through no fault of their own, are laid off or made redundant are not made to feel that their working life has been in vain.

The drive to cut costs has generated deep job insecurity and economic anxiety, which ultimately permeates the whole fabric of society. Hostility between management and workers has been fuelled by statistics that show CEO salaries increasing rapidly in parallel with stagnant salaries and layoffs. The conference organised by President Clinton with the top 100 CEOs in the United States focused on the unwritten social contract of mutual loyalty between employers and employees. There are of course sound political benefits in encouraging employers to treat their workers well. CEOs have been clear to emphasise that the provision of benefits to workers springs not from the goodness of their hearts but because shoddy treatment of employees damages loyalty and productivity of workers. The *Wall Street Journal* has reported many instances where major US companies have been burned by decisions to lay off large numbers of workers. Large-scale cost cuttings backfired, profits tumbled, customer relationships became strained and employees became demoralised. Even relatively small cost cutting by companies can have detrimental effects. Press reports of the restructuring by Digital Equipment Corporation, which saw it cut hundreds of jobs in its health-care group, resulted in many of the laid-off workers going to Digital's competitors and taking clients with them. Continental Airlines once decided to remove aspirin on its flights in order to save $25,000 a year only to have it backfire when angry customers complained heavily about the lack of headache relief on Continental flights. Such activities are the opposite of praise. They downgrade the needs of workers and customers.

Many CEOs have also realised that the cost of improving the conditions of workers can be less than the cost of losing those workers. Yvon Choinard, the founder of the outdoor-wear maker Patagonia, is on record for saying that allowing workers, including mothers, to have their young children by their sides as they worked fostered loyalty to the company, which in turn was good for business. Feeling valued for whatever reason by your employer is a form of praise. Choinard stated, 'We don't provide these benefits because we're nice. We provide them because they are good for our business. It is linked — quality product, quality customer service, quality workplace, quality of life of your employees, even quality of life for all living things on this planet — if you miss any one piece, there's a good chance you'll miss it all'.

If you want to know more about your employers, check out the toilets. A well-known Sydney radio station, which was notorious for its cost-cutting, including never having the carpets cleaned, irregular cleaning of toilets, a disease-ridden kitchen for staff, never understood how these actions were linked to its low ratings. What happens in the workplace is always reflected in what happens on the microphone. People who are forced to work in such depressing environments will carry this even in the tone of their voices on air. Managers who understand that corporate responsibility produces better results in the workplace will be the winners.

Being a bastard can be bad not just for your colleagues but bad for business. So too can excluding women and people from different ethnic backgrounds from your company. Robert Joss, an American banker who came from California in 1993 to become Managing Director of Westpac in Australia, was struck by the overriding white, male culture. At his first meeting in Sydney with 100 bankers he was stunned by its lack of diversity. Everyone looked like him. He says it 'makes business sense to have your staff reflect your customer base'. He also thinks that 'unbusinesslike habits develop if the workforce is dominated by one race or gender'.

People who are excluded from developing their full talents and potential because of their gender or their ethnic background feel undervalued. Companies who fail to recognise this will lose the talents of its potential workforce. Those who do recognise this will be ahead in terms of competition. You can no longer succeed by recognising the talents of only half the population. As the world begins to trade across more national and cultural borders, management needs to be more accepting of different leadership styles, ethnicities and genders. This is already happening in Europe because of the monetary union.

Deep down, we all know that notions of one ethnic group being superior to another or men being superior to women, are false. It is useful for people who have had no successes in life and therefore no praise to look down on someone. People who think that life has delivered them a raw deal are often the most racist and sexist in their attitudes.

To be racist is to be less than fully human.
To be sexist is to be less than fully human.

Praise helps people to grow beyond racist or sexist limitations. Praise helps people discover the possibilities of their knowledge and their experience. You have to learn how to praise yourself for doing a good job too. There's no such thing as a perfect job but your attitude towards doing any job is what counts. If you value yourself you will always try and do your best, regardless of the task.

> *The thing is that work ought to be enjoyable just because it's work. You should discipline yourself to enjoy what you do. Even if it's peeling potatoes. One of the things I notice all the time is that no matter what people do, they want it always to be this, that, and the other thing. I try to tell people that, no matter what you do for a living, it's 90 per cent shit. The most perfect and paradisiacal job in the world is still 90 per cent shit. You do the 90 per cent shit to have the 10 per cent gold. When you're writing a novel, typing those million or however many words you do from the first draft to the last, it's tiring! There's a lot of shit work. What turns you on is the sheer satisfaction of having created something out of nothing, then polishing it until it shines.*
> COLLEEN MCCULLOUGH *Tall Poppies Too*

> *I would not describe myself as ambitious. Ambition is more artificial. I would describe myself as blooming. I mean the self that I feel in myself is one*

*that blooms rather than climbs. You have to set
some goals, you have to say, 'Well, I'm going to
work on this book for a year, two years at the most,
because of contracts and deadlines'. So you have to
have order, but in terms of just being ambitious, I
mean, why would I be ambitious? Because
competitively I don't feel that.*

ALICE WALKER *Icons, Saints and Divas*

No-one feels valued any more in the workplace.

What is needed is a cultural change. Now the general rule is that if you don't receive any negative feedback you are meant to assume that you are doing a good job. The absence of criticism is the only form of praise that most workers receive.

A culture of praise must be fostered at all levels of the workplace. Everyone must be made aware of the importance of receiving personal recognition for their efforts. Begin today. Send someone you work with an email or a fax or a note or 'a golden nugget' of praise. If they comment on it in a suspicious way, explain why you are changing the culture.

Emphasise that praise is not flattery, it is not manipulative or a seductive form of power. It is a golden nugget of truth. When you receive it, treasure it as you would a nugget of gold, keep it in your pocket for when times are mean or lean.

11

HEALTH: ENERGY
OF PRAISE

* Stress
* Diet
* Relaxation
* Procrastination
* Decision-making

Positive thinking is a form of self-praise because it means that you believe in yourself and your ability to overcome obstacles. Many books have been written about how the mind is so closely linked with the body that it can actively affect its level of health.

While there is as yet no body of scientific evidence for this, medical researchers are focusing on it. New research suggests that women with breast cancer who remained optimistic and minimised the disease's impact on their lives survived twice as long as those who were overwhelmed by it. Results from a five-year study of eighty-six Sydney women with advanced breast cancer showed that those who could limit its impact had a better quality of life and survived on average 2.25 years, that is about a year longer than those who were overwhelmed by the disease. A six-year study of 116 patients with melanoma by the same researchers found that those who were optimistic and able to minimise the impact of cancer also had a better quality of life and survived longer. Future research will focus on whether patients who have a positive outlook have an improved immune response and produce more or less stress hormones — which could ultimately influence the progression of the cancer and the patient's survival.

Whatever the ultimate scientific explanation, it is clear that approaching any disease or illness with a positive outlook rather than a fearful or negative one is beneficial. However, there is a danger that people whose illness does not improve feel that they are to blame for not thinking positively enough, for not fighting hard enough. Blame is a negative force and people can only do what they are capable of achieving. Praise and encouragement will help them to keep going and not give up.

Dr Herbert Spiegal, a New York City psychiatrist, tells this true story as a dramatic example of how negative beliefs, whether expressed by yourself or someone else, can have a frightening impact on your health. A patient in a cardiac ward in a Catholic hospital took a turn for the worse and was about to die. Doctors called a priest to administer last rites. The priest mistakenly gives them to the not-so-sick patient in the next bed who dies within 15 minutes. Named the nocebo effect, the opposite of the placebo effect (positive thinking can improve your health), this phenomenon has traditionally explained everything from voodoo death, the Aboriginal punishment of 'pointing the bone' and familiar stories of medical students who develop the illnesses they study. Dr Herbert Benson, Associate Professor of Medicine at Harvard Medical School, claims that 60–90 per cent of common medical conditions can be exacerbated by the nocebo effect, for example, chest pain, headache, asthma and conditions which may not have a specific cause. Such ailments can be influenced by stress, which in turn can be influenced by our thoughts.

Although scientists cannot yet pinpoint how negative thoughts may contribute to illness, brain research is revealing that areas of the brain where fear is expressed are connected to places in the brain that directly affect key organs, such as the heart. If a person is afraid, the fear could trigger life-threatening irregular heartbeats.

We all know these things instinctively. If we wake up in the morning feeling negative and depressed we can actually begin to feel unwell. If we force ourselves to get up, think positively and get on with life we forget about our aches and pains. The real challenge is how to turn negative energy into positive energy.

John Newcombe, the Australian tennis legend, former world number one tennis player and winner of seven Grand Slam titles including three Wimbledon championships, remembers receiving a call when he was 18 from a spectator called James Doon who had watched him through binoculars when he was playing in Sydney. James Doon was a sports psychologist who later taught Newcombe a range of exercises and techniques whereby he could turn the negative into the positive. One of the exercises required Newcombe to stand on the roof of a building in Kings Cross with a clear view of the Harbour Bridge. Newcombe reports, 'I would close my eyes and feel I was reaching out and grabbing each end of the Harbour Bridge and lifting it out of the water, then putting it back again. I really thought I had the bridge coming out of the water'. When asked what it felt like, he said, 'Power. Powerful. If I set my mind to do anything, I could do it'.

Another exercise which Newcombe says he now uses when he is coaching Australian Davis Cup players is to get them to go to the court where they are playing the next day, go to the back of the stand, look down on the court and imagine that they are enveloping it. When they close their eyes they can imagine that the court and them are one.

It was, however, Newcombe's mother Lillian who, without the knowledge of the sports psychologist, somehow knew instinctively how to teach him to turn his negative energy into positive energy. He said that when he was a child he was prone to tantrums and would run into his bedroom and slam the door. After a while, he said, Lillian would come and sit on his bed and talk to him. Gradually, as she spoke to him, time after time over the years, 'the rock of temper softened into the clay of resolve'. He now realises that his mother had the wisdom to see that his very strong spirit could be used negatively or positively in his life.

As a player Newcombe genuinely believes that he conquered the fear of winning or losing that is at the core of every professional tennis player. After his playing career ended he took those beliefs and used them in his life away from the court.

James Doon also attached wires to Newcombe to measure stress levels and pulse rate. They would then talk about different players and different subjects and the device would reveal when he was experiencing fear. They would then keep talking about it until the needle moved back out of the red fear zone.

This method of talking someone through a fear is of course used by rescue and emergency workers on a daily basis, but it can be used for all aspects of your life, no matter how trivial. If you don't have anyone else with you to reinforce the positive and dispel your fears then you have to give the same talk to yourself inside your own head. Probably your worst nightmare would be to find yourself in a situation like Victoria Friend who, after a plane crash, lay near the dead body of her boyfriend for 43 hours with third-degree burns, maggots eating her flesh, exposed to the Australian sun's summer heat by day and the chill-to-the-bone cold at night. Somehow she survived and even managed to say 'thank you' to her rescuers.

How did she survive when most people would have perished? Apart from the fact that she was physically fit, Dr Yugon Mendalier, Director of Westmead Hospital's intensive care unit where Ms Friend was taken, believes that it's the psychological will to survive that makes all the difference. You have to believe in yourself, believe in your own capacity to survive. Ms Friend's personality or strength of character helped her to conserve bodily fluids despite being considerably dehydrated. Dr Mendalier is reported as saying that being high-spirited, boisterous, having friends, enjoying living and having a tenacity for life were also important factors. Ms Friend fitted this profile.

Consulting psychologist Fred Orr agreed that the fighting spirit people possessed could double their chances of survival. He said, 'having taken the step of deciding you're going to live, you then become focused and task-oriented by making sure you have a plan of action...'. 'For Victoria,' Dr Orr said, 'that must have been getting clear of the plane, deciding to stay with the wreckage, lying still to conserve energy and staying calm and composed enough to thank her rescuers'. Similar calm thinking and absence of panic was evident in the 1997 Thredbo disaster victim Stuart Diver who survived 65 hours in a freezing, flooded tomb buried underground, and student James Scott who weathered 43 days in an ice cave in the Himalayas in 1992.

Professor Dunn at Royal North Shore Hospital in Sydney, who is running a six-year research project on how important the spirit of survival is to cancer patients, says, 'It's simply that people decide they are not ready to die and think of practical ways of helping themselves. The evidence is increasing that the cluster of psychological factors around wanting to live are very important'.

*Although none of the oncologists I had met had
offered me real hope and most were negative about
my chances, I decided I had one chance out of five.
I simply made it up.
By the time I got home that afternoon, I had utterly
obliterated the word 'terminal' from my memory. I
never used it in describing my illness to people, and
indeed, when doctors I encountered a year or two
later acted astonished at meeting someone who had
survived esophageal cancer, I did not understand
their shock. I had managed to forget totally that my
cancer had been terminal; indeed, I had never
absorbed the fact that no one survives metastasized
esophageal cancer. I cancelled this fact for myself
and for everyone I spoke to. In fierce blind
insistence, I decided I had a chance to survive and
would count on that. I might as well be part of the
one as part of the other four, I told everyone,
deeding them all my wilful delusion. Within a*

couple of days, I had changed the figure to one out of four. By then, I had also repressed any sense that I was deluding myself.

This was strange, because I am and have been all my life a person who demands the truth, no matter how unpleasant it may be. I speak it and want to hear it spoken, even at the risk of being confrontational. I have contempt for wishful thinking and comforting illusions, and I despise people who are too timorous to face hard truths. Yet here I was, lying to myself and everyone else.

In fact, hope makes the ordeal of cancer treatment a little more bearable; it provides a basis for feeling a bit of cheer each day. No one who is diagnosed as having cancer fails to be aware that death may be imminent, is indeed more probable than survival; people expect to die even if their doctors offer hope: few cancer patients are overly optimistic, no matter how macho their talk. My doctors were not positive. I suppose doctors deny hope because they do not want to be accused of offering false hope (or sued for it, perhaps), but I think they should refrain from smashing what hope a patient may stubbornly cling to.

Throughout my treatment for cancer, I not only maintained false hope but denied the reality I had briefly been aware of, the terminal nature of my disease. At no time was I unaware that I would probably die within the year — I had revised my will even before I saw the new oncologist. My mind refused to budge very far, to entertain thoughts of the future beyond a few hours thence. Yet at the same time I felt insistently that I had a chance to live.

MARILYN FRENCH *A Season in Hell*

Deciding that you want to live, that you are not ready to die is deciding that you have some value, that you value yourself and your life or that other people like your friends and your family would be bereft without you, so you must continue to live. Being valued and feeling this, is a form of praise.

What keeps people wanting to live? This is the question that needs to be asked, particularly in the face of the alarming increase in the number of teenage suicides. Why do many young people who go through tough times not want to kill themselves? I believe the answer is that they feel valued and have the belief that they will come through these tough times. Those around them must continue to instil this positive belief in them, no matter how long it takes or how many mistakes they make along the way.

Psychiatrists in Hobart studied the crew of a small cargo ship that sank off the south-west coast of Tasmania in 1977. The ten men drifted in cold, rough seas for nine days until they reached a rocky beach. It was reported that during their ordeal their leader insisted they talk only positively. Maintaining belief in their survival and focusing on reunion with their loved ones helped all of them survive, except for one man who was described by the others as having 'given up'. He died on the raft on the fifth day.

The way to instil this kind of self-belief and strength of thinking in young people, despite the prevalent mood of cynicism and hopelessness promoted by an exploitative music industry, is to create a sea change in our culture. We need a culture of praise, support and positive encouragement. Young people, no matter how difficult, stubborn or infuriating, and they can be all of these, must always be reinforced by praise or by being helped to find something for them to do whereby they can begin to believe in themselves.

Most people, no matter how hopeless their lives seem, want to survive.

Jane Campion's mother was depressed most of Jane's young life. At one stage she told her mother she would understand if she wanted to end all the pain. Her mother's response was 'No'. She wanted to live, not die. Campion said, 'I realised that my job was not to see her darkness but say "it's going to get better"'.

I'm not sure whether the story about the man who cured himself of cancer by continuously watching Marx Brothers movies, causing himself to laugh a lot, is true or an urban myth but there is a growing body of evidence that laughter medicine or 'gelatology' is becoming a serious science in the US. Media medico, Dr James Wright, says that humour centres are being set up in US hospitals and health-care centres. 'Laughter requires the co-ordinated movement of fifteen facial muscles. It improves blood flow and neoxygenates all body organs which causes improved movement of nutrients, oxygen and removal of metabolic toxins.' He said that it had been in use for centuries as a serious scientific method but was a relatively young science in Western cultures.

Laughter therapists recently convened a seminar at the University of Sydney, teaching health and social welfare workers how to use humour to boost the wellbeing of themselves and their clients. Humour can help them deal with their own work stresses and relieve anxiety. If they can help a patient joke about themselves, they can help them see that they are more than their illness. Many adults can also rediscover humour from watching children who usually don't do anything unless it's fun.

Humour therapy using laughter as a cathartic response can also allow the use of grief. Tears of laughter can sometimes result in the release of deep sorrow. Collect a stack of videos of films and television series that make you laugh and play them regularly for your health. Give yourself a treat or share the laughter with someone with the same sense of humour. If you need it, do it now. Don't think about it. Act.

One of the biggest problems that confronts us today is that of addiction or dependence on substances that are bad for us. This can range from everyday struggles with diet or cigarettes to major struggles against alcohol, drugs or gambling. We all have bad habits, it's just a question of degree.

Freeing people from major life-threatening addictions is a big industry and there are so many experts in the field that I couldn't possibly cover the topic properly in this book. On a personal level I have waged a successful battle against smoking. I continue to wage a not-so-successful battle against overeating. Fortunately, I have never become addicted to alcohol or gambling, although I have friends who have. Some of these have lost their marriages, their professions and ended up in gaol. There is a restlessness in addictive or obsessive people and they have to learn to use that energy to create rather than destroy. They have to teach themselves to turn that negative energy into positive action. One of them told me how every day in gaol he started to toughen himself up. He would exercise for a set amount of time. He would go without cigarettes or chocolates and little by little develop a tough mind-set, a discipline. He taught himself to become obsessive about not indulging himself in something harmful rather than obsessing on indulging it. Day by day, he changed the habit of indulgence to the habit of denial and praised himself for every small effort. If he slipped back he didn't berate himself or give up, he just talked to himself and got back on track. Some people have to reach rock bottom before they force themselves to take control of their addiction. They never recover fully. As Alcoholics Anonymous teaches them, they are always to think of themselves as 'recovering alcoholics'. By sharing their personal stories at AA meetings they not only feel less alone but are sustained by the support and praise of the other members. No-one ever gives up on them, no matter how many times they slip back to their old habits. Never giving up on someone, always believing in them is the highest form of praise.

What I have learnt from personal and sometimes bitter experience is that you can't 'save' people who are addicted. All you can do is encourage them to save themselves by doing something about their problem. They must personally seek help and be allowed to fail and pick themselves up and try again. The best help you can give them is to praise their efforts, no matter how imperfect, and let them know that you believe in their efforts to take control of their own life.

On a personal level, at the time of writing this book my battle with my weight continues, particularly as writing is a very sedentary and mentally tiring occupation. I have visited the doctor, my cholesterol is too high. I know for the sake of my health, I must develop some discipline with my eating and do some exercise. So I have to practise what I am preaching. It's hard. But I am encouraged by people like Oprah Winfrey who has waged a similar battle with her weight openly and honestly in front of twenty million viewers around the world. Admittedly I, like most people, don't have the funds for a personal trainer or chef but I know that despite this, the real battle is waged inside each person's head.

Roseanne Barr, another television performer whom I admire, has also been honest with her viewers. She admitted that she knew she was losing the mental war and made the decision, after a great deal of soul searching, to take the risk of stomach surgery. For some people this is the only answer. It is not without its dangers and it is far better to be able to discipline yourself to eat small amounts of food but in her case she had to seek more drastic help. And it has worked. The point is she didn't give in.

Both Oprah and Roseanne have used their fame and celebrity and their money to present shows that have a positive impact on the lives of their viewers. Unlike shows that feed voyeuristically on people's afflictions, problems and aberrations, Roseanne and Oprah, having stated the problem and allowed people to tell their stories, always attempt to teach people how to deal with them.

Their programs praise their audience and their viewers because they are based on a belief that human beings can take positive control of their lives. They attempt to help themselves and us to grow. Oprah, in particular, has focused her programs on spiritual growth.

M. Scott Peck, author of *The Road Less Travelled,* makes no distinction between the mind and the spirit and therefore no distinction between the process of achieving spiritual growth and achieving mental growth. Oprah sets up the problems in life that we all face and has an expert or a series of experts to help her guests solve them, thereby enabling them to transcend them and to grow mentally and spiritually.

Peck begins his phenomenally successful book by reminding us that 'life is a series of problems. Do we want to moan about them or solve them? Do we want to teach our children to solve them?'

How often have we been asked for help by a friend only to have every suggestion for solving the problem dismissed. You can't help someone if they don't really want to help themselves. All you can do is say something like, 'I'm sure that when you are ready to solve this problem you will do it' thereby demonstrating your belief in their own ability to deal with it.

Peck reminds us that 'it is in this whole process of meeting and solving problems that life has meaning. Problems are the cutting edge that distinguishes between success and failure. Problems call for our courage and wisdom; indeed they create our courage and wisdom ... It is through the pain of confronting and resolving problems that we learn.'

So often I have said to myself, 'Why do I only learn from my failures? Why can't I learn from my successes?' The truth is that's how everyone learns. Wise people have not only had more failures because they have taken more risks but they have confronted their problems and learnt from them.

Most of us in our effort to avoid pain attempt to avoid our problems in the hope that they will go away. We are very inventive in our avoidance. Peck, who is a psychotherapist, believes that 'this tendency to avoid problems and the suffering inherent in them is the primary basis of all human mental illness'. It therefore follows that the better you are at confronting your problems and dealing with their attendant pain the more mentally healthy you are.

One of the biggest problems that most of us avoid facing is old age. As the baby boomer generation begins to enter what has become known as the older generation these problems will reach epidemic proportions. Most of us are scared of being old because we fear that we will somehow be lesser, we will be treated differently and we will be less powerful in deciding how our life is lived. Given that life expectancy is increasing every decade and barring debilitating illness, most of us will have at least twenty years with the tag of 'old' hanging over our heads.

Jeanne Calment is the world's oldest person, having lived longer than 120 years. Researchers who work on how to extend the human lifespan have analysed all aspects of her life. She was not athletic in her youth, nor a health fanatic. She gave up smoking her two cigarettes a day when she was 117 and when she was 119 she gave up her daily glass of port.

She said she enjoyed everything, has spent her life with a smile on her face and expects to 'die laughing'. The latest American research believes this may in fact be the key to her longevity. Mood can affect the immune system and changing emotional behaviour and outlook may be just as important in maintaining good health as giving up smoking or losing weight. Now that's a comfort isn't it? Of course, it doesn't have to be an either/or choice, but if the reports are to be believed, changing your attitude as well as your behaviour could add years to your life.

A twenty-two-year study of 750 white middle-class men now aged about 70, showed that 'socially dominant men, the type most likely to monopolise conversations, interrupt others and constantly compete for attention, were significantly more likely to die earlier than their more relaxed counterparts'.

Barbara Cartland, the world's oldest and most prolific author — she writes a book a fortnight — believes that staying active is part of the secret of living life to the full. She said, 'You can't stop your body growing old, but your brain can remain young forever'.

Raymond Keene, chess grandmaster and co-author of *The Age Heresy*, says 'never retire. If you finish one job, start another. Get an allotment or take a degree in philosophy — whatever interests you and will keep your brain active. Once the brain stops working, it shuts down surprisingly fast'.

Keene believes that, contrary to the popular belief that we lose brain cells every day, by taking up 'mind sports', like chess or a musical instrument and practising on a daily basis, it is possible to strengthen the brain.

If our attitude towards ageing is inextricably linked to our general attitude to life, then believing that ageing is nothing to fear, that it is something to be enjoyed like the rest of your life, that life is always an adventure and full of possibilities if you are open to them, is also a form of praise. Giving yourself the right to feel good no matter what your age, is clearly a key to a long life.

Look at the fascinating research coming out of
England at the moment about getting ninety-year-
olds to do aerobics. It's unbelievable. Within six
weeks they have increased their muscle strength by
30 per cent; people who were in wheelchairs are able
to get out of them; people who were walking with
sticks are walking without. Because we think we're
old, because we think we're sick, or female, or male,
or fat, thin, short, tall, the first child, the last child,
or have a criminal record, that's how we cripple
ourselves. You can really push that to one side and
think, 'What do I want to be?' When you say that to
yourself you start to be creative.

FABIAN DATTNER *Tall Poppies Too*

A child wakes up every day expecting to enjoy it and, because life
is so full of wonder and if the child is loved and encouraged to
explore new experiences, usually does. A person at the end of their
life should approach it in the same way and be encouraged to do
so, no matter how small or trivial the pleasure.

In 1960, at the age of 76, Eleanor Roosevelt in her collection of
reflective essays *You Learn by Living*, described herself as an
'adventurer'.

There is no experience from which you can't learn
something ... And the purpose of life, after all, is to
live it to taste experience to the utmost, to reach out
eagerly and without fear for newer and richer
experience.
You can do that only if you have curiosity, an
unquenchable spirit of adventure. The experience
can have meaning only if you understand it. You
can understand it only if you have arrived at some
knowledge of yourself, a knowledge based on a
deliberately and usually painfully acquired self-

> *discipline, which teaches you to cast out fear and*
> *frees you for the fullest experience of the adventure*
> *of life ...*

Many older people are fearful of the pace of technological change in the world and are not encouraged to become part of it. One of the young men who has undertaken the sometimes difficult task of teaching me how to make the best use of my computer and the Internet despite my exhortations regarding my age, told me not to despair. His best student was 81. He said she was living in a retirement village and was totally bored. So she left, bought herself a small cottage and rang up his computer firm. She told him, 'I want you to sell me a computer and show me how to get on the Internet.'

According to my teacher she has never looked back. Her days are full of the most exciting journeys to the best galleries in the world. She reads the New York Times and The Times in London every day with her breakfast. Every day is one of discovery for her.

> *My memory improves the older I get. Most people*
> *get lazy. Speaking as a neurophysiologist, unless one*
> *develops Alzheimer's or something, you should be*
> *able to improve. You don't use all that stuff up*
> *there. Nobody does. So you should be able to open*
> *up new pathways all the time. And that's what I do.*
> COLLEEN MCCULLOUGH *Tall Poppies Too*

To encourage an older person to continue to learn, to grow, to pursue whatever it is they like to do is no different from the kind of praise we give young people.

We should also hug and kiss older people as often as we do younger ones. So often you see children giving their older parents a perfunctory kiss. Nothing is more praiseworthy than a big hard hug. Or holding their aged and mottled hands. We know that babies who aren't hugged or stroked can physically wither and die but the same is true of old people.

The test of a good nursing home for the aged is the number of times the staff touch the patients. I knew my father was in a good place when I saw the staff hold the patients' hands when they talked to them and physically hug them. No matter how decrepit or repulsive you may feel your body has become, if someone else touches it warmly, you never feel as badly. A big hard hug is a very important form of praise for everybody, no matter what age or gender. Men should practise hugging their sons and their fathers on a daily basis. If girls never stop kissing and hugging their parents, why should boys?

The saddest part of Germaine Greer's life as she told it in her book *Daddy, We Hardly Knew You* was that her father never hugged her. Not once in her entire life. Instead she took joy and comfort from music and poetry. When she graduated from Oxford University, there was no praise from her parents.

When I came up to Cambridge my fellow-students were showing their parents around their rooms, the lecture theatres, the Backs, posing for pictures in the family album. The families beamed with pride and pleasure, shouted and ran about, gathering images of their successful children against the background of Erasmus' bridge and the Wren Library and the stone nougat of King's College. Nobody photographed me, not then, not when I knelt resplendent in medieval red and black with my hands joined in prayer within those of the Vice Chancellor, Germaine Greer Philosophiae Doctoris Cantabrigiensis. I collected my degree by myself. There was no victory supper, no champagne. I had worked all my life for love, done my best to please everybody, kept on going till I reached the top, looked about and found I was all alone. My parents were too ignorant even to appreciate what I had achieved. I thanked my lucky stars it was English

*poetry I studied, so that I had the charms and
incantations to lay upon the wound in my soul. If I
had chosen to study dentistry or computer science, I
might never have won through to happiness.*

Hug something to yourself that you value, that uplifts you, and it
will sustain you and give you a sense of being 'fully alive'. If it
can't be people, then let it be music or poetry or art.

12

THE PRAISE CLEANSING DIET

In only one month you will feel taller, thinner, healthier, wittier, happier and sexier.

WEEK ONE
Day One
Sing under the shower.
Hum your favourite tune all day.
Tell yourself what you are good at.
Tell yourself your best features.
Use superlatives.

Day Two
Tell someone else how good they are. It doesn't matter who it is.
Smile at everyone you make eye contact with.
Use superlatives.

Day Three
Write down some key words that will remind you to laugh.
Put this golden nugget of laughter in your pocket.
Watch a film or a video that makes you laugh.
Give yourself a treat.
Use superlatives.

Day Four
Look in the mirror and tell yourself how sexy you are.
Tell someone else something you did that was great.
Send yourself a fax or an email or a thank you note.
Use superlatives.

Day Five
Put a golden nugget of praise in your child's lunchbox or schoolbag.
Put a golden nugget of praise under your lover's pillow.
Send or buy someone some flowers.
Use superlatives.

Day Six
Do one thing you've never done before.
Tell someone a joke or a funny story.
Hug or hold the hands of an old person.
Write, fax or email praise to someone.
Use superlatives.

Day Seven
Write down a list of things you wish you'd done.
Do one of them or take a step towards it.
Tell someone you love how much you love them.
Tell someone at work how much you appreciate them.
Wear a funny hat.
Use nothing but superlatives.

At the end of the week, if your friends and colleagues haven't suggested you visit a shrink, tell them why you were practising praise. Notice how infectious it is.

Week Two
Do it all again. Only more boldly.

Week Three
Have fun. Be wild. Let yourself go. Laugh a lot.

Week Four
Make it up yourself.

13

CHANGE AND RISK: FROM PRAISE TO BOLDNESS

*   Imagination
*   Time
*   Information
*   Optimism/Pessimism
*   Denial

When we are children, the statement 'I dare you' takes on tremendous power and importance. It also excites you. For in that excitement is the possibility that by taking on that dare, by taking a chance, leaping into the unknown, you may succeed in doing something you have never previously tried. What stops you or paralyses you is the fear that you may fail, that others will know that you have failed and mock you.

The child that learns to deal with jeering and mocking with the retort, 'Well at least I tried, which is more than you did', is the child that is learning not to be afraid of risking and, more importantly, failing. This is the child that will ultimately succeed in whatever they choose.

By taking risks I don't mean being reckless, especially in terms of purposely endangering your life. Sometimes just getting in your car, or catching a plane or crossing the road is endangering your life. Life is terrifying, if you stop to consider it.

Any change involves risk but we live in times that are changing rapidly, whether we like it or not. Again, we have a choice. We can choose to embrace the new technological world, and of course that means that we will fail from time to time or even appear to make fools of ourselves but so what. Every time you take a risk or make a change, say to yourself so what if I don't succeed the first time. So what! Will the world stop?

When I was a university lecturer I would often be visited by people in their fifties or sixties who would enquire about some of the courses I was teaching. When I explained that they would have to enrol in a three-year degree they would say, 'But that's too long. I will (for example), be 53 when I finish'. And I would say to them, 'Well, how old will you be in three years' time if you don't do it?' And then they would say, 'But what if I fail?' And I would remind them of the 'So What?' test.

The real tragedy is not in trying and failing, it's in never having tried. None of us knows what we can achieve until we try. And that involves taking a bit of a risk.

The real task if you want to try something but fear prevents you from ever taking the first step, is to imagine you're doing it. Call it visualisation or just daydreaming but sit down or lie down and let your imagination do the work. Repeat this every day until you can take the first step towards the change you want to make in your life. It was one of the world's great thinkers, Einstein, who said, 'Imagination is more important than knowledge'.

If you start every day by imagining yourself doing something you have always secretly wanted to do but allowed your fear of change to prevent you, then even to imagine yourself doing it is a form of praise. It is a reminder that you are capable of more than you know.

So often people say, 'I'd like to change or take that risk but it's not the right time'. There is no right or wrong time, there is just your own fear or your own negativity. Sometimes when everything is in place and you are feeling on top of things, the next move is obvious. But what about when you are in the middle of a big set-back and all you can see ahead is failure and gloom. This is very often the best time to work out what it is you really want from life. Every set-back provides you with an opportunity. Particularly with an opportunity to learn.

When we are at high school and write earnest essays on Shakespeare's tragedies, particularly plays like *Hamlet* or *King Lear*, we inevitably conclude that real wisdom only comes through suffering. When we grow up, we learn that it's true. And after we have been through all the 'why me' and 'it's all so unfair' stages, we finally have to decide the kind of attitude we will take towards this suffering. Will we see it as a valuable learning experience, something that forces us to face up to what really does matter in our lives or will we allow it to make us bitter and resentful of those who are successful?

The great psychoanalyst Jung places 'synchronicity' high on his list of things that we should pay attention to, and since I have been writing this book I have been amazed at the number of times the right people have turned up in my life to help me at the right time. The right books or articles have suddenly caught my attention. Obviously these things have been happening all my life but I have not been paying attention.

For example, when I was writing my first book, *Tall Poppies,* one of the nine women on whom the book was based suddenly got cold feet about exposing the personal details of her life and pulled out. I tried to talk her around but to no avail.

By chance, or what I thought then was a lucky coincidence, I read in the newspaper that Maggie Tabberer, the fashion icon, was giving a speech at a nearby hotel. I just picked up the phone, rang the hotel, introduced myself, told her the truth about my situation and she agreed to be in the book. She said later she was so stunned by my honesty she said 'yes'. That was the beginning of a life-long friendship where we have come in and out of each other's lives at crucial times. I was the catalyst in persuading her to write her autobiography, which became a record-breaking best-seller.

Whether this is pre-destined or luck or chance or good Karma, I don't know. But I do think that opportunity and taking a risk often leads to synchronicity. So many opportunities cross our paths and if we are to make the most of them we have to be confident enough to take a chance or a risk.

It's not so much a matter of courage but of being bold. It was bold of me to ring Maggie Tabberer directly, rather than going through her agent. But so what. She was either going to say yes or no. That particular opportunity would probably never have happened again.

Boldness is a mental attitude, a liberating force. It is a way of interacting with the world. I believe that you have to be bold in order to live fully, to be able to make the most of the cards that life deals you.

Sometimes, of course, fate confronts you with tragedy and disaster. But you still have a choice. You can choose how you react to it, how you deal with it.

It is possible to learn how to be bold. Bold enough to change. Bold enough to risk failure. Bold enough to pick yourself up and try again. Every creative artist knows how scary it is to step into the unknown. But they are bold enough to take a risk. Every sportsperson knows how terrifying it is to risk failing but they keep being bold enough to try.

Every time you take a risk and you survive, even if you don't succeed, you start to build up resilience.

Being bold does not mean that you are not afraid. It means that you face up to that fear and keep going. By giving something a go you gradually learn to be bolder and less afraid. To live boldly is to be fully alive, to experience the full range of emotions.

Praise is the bedrock of boldness. Every time you praise another human being or give them respect and recognition for something they have done, you strengthen their ability to live fully. You strengthen their ability to take risks, to change, to grow.

Ask yourself why you so often hold back from giving praise. Does it make you feel vulnerable? Do you think you have never received the kind of recognition you deserve, so why should you give it to others? Do you save it up for the right time? Why can't you just give it freely and spontaneously? Does it cost you anything?

If you are mean with giving praise or recognition to others, are you also mean with giving it to yourself? Why not give it as generously to yourself as you give it to others?

If someone praises you, do you really hear it or dismiss it? Perhaps you don't even listen to it. Are you afraid you will be embarrassed by it? Are you suspicious of it? Are you scared you will get big-headed?

Praise and recognition make you bold. It is the kind of boldness that allows you to admit that you did hurt someone. It allows you to say, 'I am so sorry. What can I do to make you feel better?'

If you constantly criticise someone, particularly a child, it gives them no room to change themselves. A child particularly has no defences against criticism except blaming others. Adults who do this have usually been criticised a lot as children.

To ask someone to be aware of what they have done to harm or hurt someone else and to take responsibility for it is a form of praise. It assumes that they can learn from this admission and it assumes that they can change. It is important that you address their behaviour, not brand them.

For example, if a child hurts a cat, rather than calling the child cruel, it is better to say something like, 'I know you are really a kind person but when you do that to the cat it hurts the cat — see how it cries'. Never brand or label a child, as so often happens in families where such labels become self-fulfilling prophecies.

Don't let other people's fears or attitudes stop you from embracing change or risks. Often people hate you to do what secretly they would love to do themselves. Instead they say 'you're too old, too fat, too fixed in your ways, too inhibited'.

Often the best time to take the risk or the leap is when you are at your lowest ebb, when your confidence has really been dented.

The year when two things that I really loved doing were taken away from me totally without my control, was just such a time for me. I was doing my usual tough talk but inside I was drowning in a sea of injustice and self-pity. I knew that in order not to go under I needed to take a leap — a huge leap, a dramatic leap. This was the year when I decided to write my first international book. Prior to this all my books had been based in Australia. I drew up a list of the women writers I most admired, the women writers whose books had changed the world and decided I would go to New York and talk to them.

I must admit that my Australian friends tried to be encouraging but would then say things like, 'Do you really think they will talk to you? They must all be so busy'.

My American friends, on the other hand, said, 'What a great idea. Go for it. I'll help you'.

And that is the kind of praise that catapults you into taking a risk. Shelley Gare, a columnist for *The Australian* newspaper writes that she 'once wrote down for a disheartened friend "Twenty things that should always make you happy" and simply listed his numerous achievements, the bare facts of his life and his special qualities'. What surprised her was 'the wonder with which he read this very obvious list about himself, and the way he revisited it a day or so later to remind himself again what he had earned in his life'.

She believes that we don't congratulate ourselves enough. We let our critics get to us. You have to take risks if you decide something is worth the effort. What amazed me about what I thought was such a big step was that it was so easy. With the help of my New York friends and their contacts I simply rang up everyone on my list and one by one they said 'Yes'. One year later I was pounding the hot streets of Manhattan and in ten days had talked to ten of the most influential writers in the world. And so my book *Icons, Saints and Divas* was written. And, as I write in the postscript, this is what I learnt.

> *These writers and their books have taught us all to*
> *ask 'How far can I go? How much can I achieve?'*
> *and to stretch the boundaries of possibility, to leap*
> *the barrier, to push out the envelope, to crack*

> *through the glass ceiling, to go where others have*
> *feared to tread. In short, they have taught us **to be***
> ***bold, not to be afraid**. As Robin Morgan's poem*
> *said, 'There is nothing you cannot be'.*

And so *Icons, Saints and Divas* became a best-seller in Australia and is published in the UK, Holland and Germany.

If I had not had those set-backs I would never have dared to take that step, nor would I have had the time to write the book.

Praise from others gave me the belief in myself to make the change from depression and self-pity to optimism and determination.

In order to take a risk you need to be able to imagine yourself doing the things that you want to do. Fantasy will always lead to reality. It is rare that we achieve something that we have not, even in our wildest dreams, imagined ourselves doing. Sometimes it is impossible to even imagine yourself getting out of a trough of despair, your confidence is so low.

Brett Kelly was a twenty-two-year old who thought of himself as someone who had always played by the rules and was working hard at being successful, until he was sacked. It was a terrible shock and he felt totally lost and without direction. He slipped into the predictable routine of sleeping in, watching daytime television and wasting the day. His friends had asked him to go skiing with them and, having at first refused, he changed his mind. He said:

> *I had committed myself to taking more risks, to be*
> *open to change, to live more for today and to just*
> *have a go.*

Taking this first decision to risk going skiing, even though he'd never skied before and had been forced to terminate his cricket ambitions because of stress fractures to his spine, was the beginning of his new life. Learning to ski by getting right behind his ski instructor and copying everything he did, started him thinking. Perhaps he could learn how to be successful in the same way. He began to write down lists of people who were successful, people he thought he could learn something from. This led to the idea of a book which would not only teach him how to be successful but help others as well.

In five days he read eight books on publishing and wrote letters to every person he wanted to meet. He thought it would be easy. But everywhere he turned he was told how and why he would fail. He was advised to get a sensible job and just 'get on with life'. He admits that every time he heard something like that it 'nibbled away' at his confidence but it also made him more determined. He did, however, get twelve interviews done in the first seven weeks and then the silence set in. The breakthrough came with his interview with Bob Hawke, a former Australian Prime Minister. What did Bob Hawke give him?

Encouragement. Which is of course a form of praise. All he needed were those words of encouragement to persist. When he came to the really difficult area of publishing he found that his confidence and commitment led him to talk to people who offered help and support. The entire process taught him some difficult truths about himself. For the first time, through interviewing people, he really learnt to listen. When I interviewed him on my radio program in Sydney after the book was published, he said that even though he had started the book wanting to find out what skills he needed to be successful, he finally realised that what made his book a reality was the support, help and goodwill of other people, this was the secret of success.

> *When I look at all the people I've interviewed, one*
> *of the things they have in common is a great skill at*
> *building relationships. They were friendly, generous*
> *and encouraging.*

He realised that he had been so busy chasing qualifications and skills that he had forgotten about the power of personal relationships.

> *You can't be successful unless relationships are the*

primary part of that success. With those relationships
you achieve more, your life is richer and more
interesting and you have a lot of fun.

Not only did young Brett Kelly get a wonderful new job but he put together and published his book *Collective Wisdom* so that others could learn from his experience. When he had been sacked it was the first time anything had really gone wrong for him. Of course he spent a while feeling sorry for himself but then he knew he had to make a change in his life and that involved taking a risk. Starting a book was a huge leap but it was the catalyst for changing his life. All he needed along the way was the enthusiasm and encouragement of other people to keep him going.

Praise does not have to be effusive or over-the-top. Sometimes just a warm word and a smile is enough. The power of other people's encouragement taught him that he too needed to be able to give that. And that success for all the people he interviewed was based on their skills at building relationships. Making someone feel good is a form of praise and the basis for all successful relationships.

Any change in one's life or one's attitudes or one's behaviour involves risk to a greater or lesser extent. Even if a person steadfastly refuses to change, the world will change and that person will become more fixed, more rigid, more isolated. In order to deal with the fear of change and its resulting sense of insecurity, you must first be able to imagine yourself in a new situation. Take a leap inside your own head. Explore all the possibilities that a change will involve. Imagine all the good and all the bad. Let your fear run free. In fact, let it run to its absurd end. And then go back and think about the positives until you become comfortable in your mind with what the change involves.

You must give yourself enough time to let your imagination take control of your fear of change or risk. So often people dismiss opportunities that stare them in the face because they never give themselves enough time to play with the idea. So much easier to quickly dismiss the opportunity out of hand.

And, having made the decision to take a risk, it is essential that you give yourself time to get used to the change. Real change takes time to bear fruit. By allowing your fear of failure to become your barometer you abandon the new before you have really given it a chance to work. Give yourself time — time to fail and pick yourself up and start again.

Successful people are successful because they have learnt from their failures and given themselves time to have another go. When you are despairing, talk to yourself. Give yourself some encouragement, some comforting words and, more importantly, give yourself time.

The word 'risk' implies a dangerous leap in the dark. As if you are being asked to close your eyes, cross your fingers, hope like hell and jump.

It is important that in order to counteract this fear you gather as much information about the area of risk that you can. So often people fail to ask questions, ask for help, and generally fail to research many areas that are new to them. People are always amazed at how willing others are to help them. Especially if you phrase the request for help in the form of praise. For example, 'You have had a lot of experience in this area and I would really value your opinion'.

> SUCCESSFUL PEOPLE ARE SUCCESSFUL BECAUSE THEY HAVE LEARNT FROM THEIR FAILURES AND GIVEN THEMSELVES TIME TO HAVE ANOTHER GO. WHEN YOU ARE DESPAIRING, TALK TO YOURSELF.

And if someone then goes on to be a great source of information, don't forget to tell them. Preferably drop them a note of thanks reinforcing how valuable their knowledge has been. Your attitude towards taking a risk is not just incidental to the outcome. Whether you are optimistic or pessimistic is intrinsic to the success of your new phase or project. Usually people resort to pessimism because it seems easier to predict that you will fail in order to minimise the disappointment and embarrassment if you do. All it does is usually become a self-fulfilling prophecy. Your attitude programs you to the result.

On the other hand, if you take a generally optimistic attitude, believing that whatever happens you will gain something from the experience and don't let the first set-back daunt you, then your optimism will eventually produce some positive results.

I'm a great believer in grabbing opportunities when they arise. I love new challenges, going to new places, meeting new people. You never know what's around the next corner. As a small child I was a great explorer. Even now, whenever I get on a plane I think, 'Who knows who I could sit next to? It could be Omar Sharif'.

SALLYANNE ATKINSON *Tall Poppies Too*

I love living in New York. It's not always good, but at other times it is fabulous. You never know what will happen next, and I love that.
When I come home to Adelaide and stay with my mother in the suburbs, I feel at ease with myself wherever I am. Sometimes while I was at Ms and going to lunch at the White House, I might think, 'What am I doing here?', but if you see life as an adventure you are open to whatever comes along. I have a great capacity for adventure.

ANNE SUMMERS *Tall Poppies Too*

All I can do is go on having the confidence to trust in my own instincts. My peace comes from continuing to have the ability and courage to make decisions. It's a dynamic life. I have people all over the world I love to spend time with. Whenever I'm in Adelaide there's a family barbecue, so I can keep in touch with my aunts and cousins. John Willett's family in London is incredibly close too. I try to see my godchildren whenever I can. Anybody that I've

ever loved I continue to love. I find my life to be
incredibly rich in people.
When my work is going well I'm happy, and when
I'm travelling I'm happy. I love to travel.
Anywhere. I love arriving somewhere new.
People want you to be what you were before. It's
quite hard to say, 'Look, I really liked doing what I
did then, and I could easily do it now, but I suspect
there's something more interesting for me to do'. I
must have the determination to give myself the
room to explore.

ROBYN ARCHER *Tall Poppies Too*

It costs no more to be optimistic than pessimistic but so often people feel that pessimism is a less threatening approach, thereby almost ensuring that the risk taking will end in gloom and doom. Sometimes people speak pessimistically in order not to sound over-confident while maintaining a quiet optimism secretly to themselves.

The point about an optimistic attitude is that it rubs off on everyone you meet. If success is essentially based on building good relationships then an optimistic attitude (even if deep down you are still a little apprehensive) will ensure the confidence and trust of other people.

By optimism I do not mean a Pollyanna style 'glad game' where you deny the reality of what is happening. If what you have attempted to do is clearly failing, for example, your new shop has no customers, then there is no point in denying that something has gone wrong. An optimistic attitude does not deny the truth, it simply means you believe that you will be able to find a solution to the problem.

The final quality you need if you are prepared to make a change or take a risk is determination. Whatever happens you must not give up. With the kind of quiet determination that Brett Kelly had to produce and publish a book, you too can overcome numerous set-backs and finally achieve your goal, whatever it is. Look at this media release that just landed on my desk.

> *First-time author Stuart Harrison has hit the jackpot*
> *with his debut novel,* The Snow Falcon, *which will*
> *be published in sixteen countries around the world*
> *and has earned him more than A$1 million in*
> *advances to date.*
> *The story of* The Snow Falcon *is a story of change and*
> *hope, much like the author's personal situation before*
> *he wrote it. The interest from publishers came just in*
> *the nick of time. 'At thirty-seven and a half, my mail*
> *order business went bust, and my wife Dale became*
> *pregnant. Realising it was now or never, I decided to*
> *follow a long-held dream of mine: to write a novel.*
> *When our baby, Mac, was four months old, Dale and*
> *I left for England. We found a remote village to live*
> *in — where it rained all the time — and I began*
> *writing. Two and a half years later I had written*
> *three novels — and all three had been rejected. I was*
> *down to my last little bit of money, before I would be*
> *forced to return to New Zealand, when I wrote a*
> *fourth, which I called* The Snow Falcon. *I knew at*
> *the end of the first draft that I had hit a vein of*
> *honesty within myself, and when, feeling foolish*
> *because my eyes had become blurry with tears, I*
> *wrote the last line, I knew also that I had found the*
> *kind of stories I wanted to write,' says Harrison.*

To be determined is the greatest praise you can give yourself. It means no matter what happens, no matter how hard it becomes, you believe in yourself. You believe that you will find a way.

> *I wasn't ever the most popular one in the class, but I*
> *always had friends. But I have never lived my life*
> *thinking I can't leave my friends, I can't leave my*
> *family, I don't know anybody in this new place. I*

have always moved for my career. Nothing else.
Making a go of it in any place is not the
responsibility of the people who live there and work
there — it's your responsibility. If you're going to
make a go of it, it's because of your own input.
COLLEEN MCCULLOUGH *Tall Poppies Too*

You must continue to think of yourself as someone who is determined, as someone who gets there in the end. Persistence and determination are not to be confused with stubbornness. People who are stubborn are those who refuse to listen. Determined people listen to those who have information and experience, they accept help, they are open to change, they are not afraid of taking risks.

Determined people are bold. And boldness always involves risk.

What are you waiting for?

When the writer and broadcaster, Robert Dessaix, was told by his doctor that he was HIV positive he reacted by doing something he had always dreamed of doing. He simply went to the airport and caught a plane and let himself be taken wherever his whim or desires took him.

The result was a book called *Night Letters* in which a man recently diagnosed with an incurable disease writes a letter home to a friend every night for twenty nights in a hotel room in Venice.

To tell you the truth, I wish I'd done it sooner. I've
lived my life far too timidly, I now think, looking
back. Not blandly, but taking too few risks. When the
road has forked, I've almost always taken the better-
lit, better-paved way, although I now suspect it's
often the other way, the grubby lane or path through
the woods, which most (I'm searching for a grittier
phrase but fear I'm left with) enrich your humanity.
ROBERT DESSAIX *Night Letters*

14

BE BOLD: CREATE YOUR
OWN LIFE

If you are going to create your own life then you have to start with yourself. Fragile, vulnerable but essentially self-determining. That's you.

Praise, learning how to give it and receive it, begins with yourself. How you describe yourself to yourself, the conversations you have with yourself, what you believe about yourself is the basis of what kind of life you will lead. It is the basis of who you are and who you will become.

Self-effacement may be culturally more acceptable than self-enhancement but it's the culture that needs to change, not you. As Nelson Mandela said in the epigraph to this book, 'Your playing small does not serve the world'.

We learn at a very young age to hide our talents, to hide our light, to hide our potential, in order that others will approve of us and not feel threatened or insecure. What we need is a cultural sea change. Praise, good old-fashioned praise, is the trigger for this change to occur. Once we give ourselves these 'nuggets of praise' we will become more generous in giving them to others. We must admit that most of us are mean with it, do not know how to give it or receive it, and yet we spend our lives craving it. When we get it and really allow ourselves to believe it, to absorb it, to let it seep into our pores, we glow. And we glow not just that one time, but every time we remember it and relive it.

A golden nugget of praise can determine the direction of your life. A golden nugget of praise has the power to change your life.

That is why we must give them to ourselves.

As Mandela said, 'We ask ourselves, "Who am I to be brilliant, gorgeous, talented and fabulous?" Actually, who are you not to be'.

Praise is the engine of self-esteem. Self-praise is not self-aggrandisement, that is puff and wind. Self-praise is reminding yourself of your light, not your darkness. Self-praise is reminding yourself of your power, not your powerlessness.

The habit of praise, like all other habits that we acquire, feeds on repetition. If you praise often enough, it becomes part of you. Whatever we give to ourselves, we give to others. Being a parent today is one of the hardest jobs we undertake. Society is changing so quickly, there are so many more agents of destruction freely available to children, like pornographic violence, drugs, evil manipulators on the Internet and some of it is very scary stuff, but simply scaring the hell out of your children about the dangers is not the only answer.

Convincing your children, however, that they are so loved and so precious to you that you don't want anything to harm them is the highest form of praise. Being a good parent is like being a good coach, the child should always know that the parent has total belief in them and wants only to bring out the best in them.

Praise them often.
Praise them generously.
Do not be afraid of superlatives.

Ban the use of the word 'quite' as in 'quite good'.
Praise will give the child a sense of their own power and their
 own creativity.

Education is the key to all learning and criticism never works. Feedback must always be framed in a positive light. Criticism stings. Criticism hurts. We withdraw from it and we resent it.

Praise will encourage people to try harder, to stretch higher, to expand their horizons. Focus on what the person can do, not what they cannot do.

Praise will enhance every relationship you have in all aspects of your life. Praise those you love at least once a day. Praise those you work with at least once a week.

Learn how to accept praise. Do not scoff or become embarrassed. Take it as graciously as you would a beautifully wrapped gift.

Learn to listen to other people. Really listen with your eyes and your ears. Listen so well you remember what is said. Listen to what the feelings are behind the words.

Remember the power of a simple 'thank you'. Write it, say it, fax it, email it. But do it.

When we work hard, we need to have it recognised, appreciated, valued. As a worker and a manager, praise is most often ignored or withheld. Take time to praise people for their work. Praise is sincere, personal and specific. It is both a validation and an inspiration. A safety net and a springboard.

Without food we die. Without praise our spirit dies. Praise is essential to good health. Praise relieves stress. Praise encourages a good diet. Praise creates relaxation. Praise gives you energy. Just as a baby needs to be admired and cuddled so too do people of all ages, especially the old. Praise strengthens our immune systems. Praise releases serotonin. Praise encourages resilience.

The power of praise makes us bold, bold enough to embrace change and take risks. Bold enough to fail and try again. Bold enough to dream and then act on those dreams. Bold enough to create our own lives, our own values, our own expectations.

As Goethe wrote:
> *Whatever you can do or*
> *dream you can, begin it.*
> *Boldness has genius,*
> *magic and power in it.*
> *Begin it now.*

Here's to your genius, magic and power.

This book is a journey, a discovery. Not just for you, I hope, but for me too. Between the years of starting and finishing it I left the university where I had lectured for twenty years of my life. During its gestation I also presented my own radio and television programs and published my eighth best-selling book. And during those years both my parents died.

With no further full-time work commitments or family responsibilities, I moved from Adelaide to Sydney and became a full-time writer and part-time broadcaster and public speaker.

I was free, finally, to create my own life. And while that freedom was exhilarating, it was also terrifying. My life and what I made of it was now up to me.

While it is true that in some senses I have already travelled a long way from where I began and have always thought of myself as the kind of person who would give most things a go, I have been forced into the realisation while writing this book that, like many others who appear to be risk-takers, I have mostly taken the well-travelled paths. Even though I have maintained an image of myself as a bold person, I have never really taken too many risks.

Unlike all my other books, except the coming-of-age novel *Hot Shots*, this book has been a risk. The real reason it has taken me years to write and finally finish it, is because I am treading, for me, a path previously untravelled.

Even though I was writing a book about being bold and being true to yourself and not worrying what other people said or how they would judge it, I found myself faltering. Not in my belief in the book's premise and content but in my ability to put myself on the line. When Gloria Steinem first completed her book *Revolution*

From Within she gave it to a close friend to read and her friend's judgement was, 'These are all good ideas but where are you in it?' And Gloria realised that she had exhibited exactly what she was writing about, she had failed to address the real person within, to confront the blocks that she had erected to keep herself and the world separate. Of course, when she did discover and write about the person within for the first time in her writer's life, she opened herself up to scornful derision and often harsh criticism. And no matter how much we say we don't care, of course we do. It hurts. Stings. But the fear of those stings and arrows should not deter us from giving something a go, from creating our own life instead of letting the opinion or judgements of others determine it.

Once, after I had given a speech, an older woman came up to me and said, 'You know I always thought that when I got older and my children had left home and my husband had died, I would wear funny hats and go to town and just have fun'.

I ALWAYS THOUGHT THAT WHEN I GOT OLDER AND MY CHILDREN HAD LEFT HOME AND MY HUSBAND HAD DIED, I WOULD WEAR FUNNY HATS AND GO TO TOWN AND JUST HAVE FUN.

'So why haven't you?' I asked.

'It all seems too late now,' she said.

'Nonsense. It's never too late. Do it tomorrow,' was my response.

And now I find that when my funny hat was this book, a book so totally different from anything else I have written, I too suffered from this cultural stumbling block — a morbid fear of really 'letting oneself go'.

In another example of synchronicity, I was recently given a biography of Gertrude Stein and Alice B. Toklas who were at the cultural heart of Paris for four decades through two world wars. They became famous simply because they were utterly true to themselves. They created their own life, with no regard for what others thought of them. As Diana Souhami, the biographer, says, they enjoyed driving around, looking at art, eating and talking. They lived well unpretentiously, and were so much themselves, people had no choice but to accept them. Both of them had a wide and eccentric collection of assorted hats which they wore for every occasion. They were without doubt a strange-looking pair.

And speaking of hats on older women, nothing could be more hilarious than the motorbike helmets worn by the late Jennifer Paterson and Clarissa Dickson Wright as they moved through the English countryside on their way to a cooking venue. *Two Fat Ladies* has been a huge success with television audiences since it began in 1996. The reason for their outstanding and surprising success, was the fact that they were absolutely and totally true to themselves. They simply didn't give a damn what anyone else thought. They were both fat, they cooked rich food, mixed it together by hand, ate beef in the land of mad-cow disease and said and did whatever they pleased. Dickson is a recovering alcoholic having inherited and blown nearly two million dollars on the high life. By her early forties she had nothing left and went back to what she knew she did well – cooking. Paterson was employed by the *Spectator* to cook lunches for executives and lost the job when she threw the dinner service out of the window in a fit of rage. They invited her back to write a cooking column instead.

The extraordinary life of each woman and their celebrity success which has happened late in their lives is due entirely to their being bold.

Bold enough to be themselves.

Bold enough to cope with whatever life dealt them.

Bold enough to believe in themselves.

Bold enough not to go along with current fashions in bodies, food, clothes.

Bold enough to never give up.

And finally, bold enough to laugh. A lot. Food was important to them and their show but so was their humour. They loved to laugh. They loved, to have a good time. They took a risk by even agreeing to put themselves up for public judgement in the cruellest and deadliest medium. But even if they had flopped, they would have laughed it off and said they at least had enjoyed themselves.

Recent research done in Australia and overseas has uncovered a demand by individuals for a more 'simple and truthful' existence. The resident futurist at one of America's foremost think-tanks, SRI Consulting, summarises the prevailing question, 'If times are so great, why do I feel so bad?'

How else to explain the proliferation of anti-depressants?

Rather than interpreting too literally people's often stated desire to return to 'traditional' values, a better word would probably be 'lasting' values. This does not mean that people want to go back to a 1950s existence, people want to move forwards, not backwards, but they do want to work out or create for themselves a life that they believe in.

GIVE YOURSELF THE RIGHT TO HAVE FUN. SELF-PRAISE IS NOT SELF-ADULATION BUT A PATHWAY TO LETTING YOURSELF GO, LETTING YOURSELF HAVE FUN. LETTING YOURSELF BE A BIT SILLY.

Australian researcher Hugh Mackay has been mapping the community's growing sense of disappointment and cynicism with institutions, particularly political institutions. This disappointment has been fuelled by lies, broken promises and poor leadership.

This has resulted in most people attempting to take their lives into their own hands. They have realised that they need to answer these questions about themselves and their lives, themselves, and not rely on institutions of Church or State to do so. American research has reinforced the general belief that most people are not prepared to trust institutions to lead them into the next century, let alone millennium. If institutions are to survive they will have to renew their own vision of what they have to offer. There is an increasing shift in power from institution and governance to individuals.

An information-based culture and economy will only reinforce the social implications of rapid change and people's need to find enduring values.

What is emerging is a new leisure class; not the traditionally wealthy, but people on smaller, dual incomes, with time for fun and leisure.

Give yourself the right to have fun. Self-praise is not self-adulation but a pathway to letting yourself go, letting yourself have fun. Letting yourself be a bit silly. Who cares what other people think. Learn to say, 'So what!' Like Gertrude Stein and Alice B Toklas, like the Two Fat Ladies you should encourage yourself to be bold enough to work out what it is you really believe in and what kind of life you want to lead. If you are sick of working too many hours and having too little fun, then get off the treadmill. Lead a simpler life. As Robin, the woman in the coffee shop underneath my apartment, constantly tells me, 'Have fun. You're a long time looking at the lid, kid'.

15

MY FATHER'S SUNROOM

Just as the death of my father catapulted me into recognising his greatest gift to me — that of praise, genuine, loving, sustaining praise — so too, by the time I finished writing this book, I realised that he was probably the happiest, most contented person I have ever known.

Happiness has become an almost meaningless word because it assumes that we all mean the same thing when we use it.

Happiness depends entirely on the way you view yourself and your life.

My father was not wealthy. Or powerful. Or ambitious. His was not a particularly easy life. His mother died when he was fifteen, his autocratic father closed up the home soon after and my father was forced to leave school, get a sales job and live in a boarding house. He survived the Depression, the battles of El Alamein and Tobruk and a wife who suffered from a lifetime of ill health.

As far as he was concerned life was pretty good if you had a roof over your head, a comfortable bed, food on the table, beer in the fridge and people you loved. Saturday meant a wad of cash in his pocket and a pie with sauce at the races with his mates. Sunday meant working in his old clothes in his vegetable garden in the morning, roast lamb for lunch, followed by an afternoon drive with the family. It certainly wasn't my dream of the good life.

After he retired, my mother decided they needed a new sunroom where they could sit and have their morning tea.

One day I arrived unexpectedly at their house to find them companionably sitting in the car, which was parked halfway down their driveway.

'What on earth are you doing?' I asked.

My father wound down his window and said cheekily, 'How do you like our new sunroom? Get in and join us'.

While I sat in the back seat of his beloved Holden he explained to me that he had worked out the perfect solution. Every morning my mother made a thermos of coffee which they took to the car together with their mugs and the cake. They had the radio tuned to their favourite station and my father moved the car up or down the drive according to the position of the sun.

'See, this way, we have our own sunroom, our morning tea, our music, heating or air-conditioning — everything we want is here. And we just follow the sun. You wouldn't be dead for quids, would you?'

I'm trying to follow his lead and be bold enough to follow my own sun. My hope is that this book helps you to follow yours.

BIBLIOGRAPHY

BAIR, Deirdre, 1990, *Simone de Beauvoir*, Jonathon Cape, London

BIDDULPH, Steve, 1995, *Manhood: An action plan for saving men's lives*, Finch Publishing, Sydney
—, 1997, *Raising Boys: Why boys are different and how to help them become happy and well-balanced men*, Finch Publishing, Sydney

BLY, Robert, 1990, *Iron John: A book about men*, Addison-Wesley, Reading

CARNEGIE, Dale, 1977, *How to Win Friends and Influence People*, Angus & Robertson, Sydney

COHEN, Herb, 1980, *You Can Negotiate Anything*, Angus & Robertson, Sydney

DESSAIX, Robert, 1998, *Night Letters*, Picador, Sydney

FRENCH, Marilyn, *A Season In Hell*, Knopf Publishing Group, New York, 1998
—, 1981, *The Women's Room*, Summit Books, New York

GREER, Germaine, 1990, *Daddy We Hardly Knew You*, Penguin Books, London

KELLY, Brett, 1998, *Collected Wisdom*, Clown, Sydney

MACKAY, Hugh, 1994, *The Good Listener*, Pan Macmillan, Sydney

MITCHELL, Susan, 1997, *Icons, Saints and Divas*, HarperCollins Australia, Sydney

—, 1984, *Tall Poppies*, Penguin, Ringwood

—, 1991, *Tall Poppies Too*, Penguin, Ringwood

—, 1987, *The Matriarchs: Twelve Australian women talk about their lives to Susan Mitchell*, Penguin, Ringwood,

—, 1986, *The Scent of Power*, Angus & Robertson, Sydney

ROBBINS, Anthony, 1992, *Awaken the Giant Within*, Simon & Schuster, New York

ROGERS, Carl, 1967, *On Becoming a Person: A therapist's view of psychotherapy*, Constable, London

SCOTT PECK, M., 1983, *The Road Less Travelled*, Arrow Books Ltd, London

SELIGMAN, Martin, 1991, *Learned Optimism*, A.A. Knopf, New York

SOUHAMI, Diana, 1993, *Gertrude and Alice*, Pandora, London

STEINEM, Gloria, 1992, *Revolution from Within*, Little, Brown & Co., Boston

WEISEN COOK, Blanche, 1993, *Eleanor Roosevelt*, Penguin, New York

ACKNOWLEDGMENTS

Grateful acknowledgment is made to the following for permission to reproduce copyright material. The publishers have made every effort to contact the holders of copyright material included in Susan Mitchell's *Be Bold and Discover the Power of Praise*. They would be pleased to hear from anyone who has not been duly acknowledged.

CHAPTER 3: extract from interview with Naomi Wolf in Susan Mitchell, *Icons, Saints and Divas*, HarperCollins Publishers, Australia, Sydney, 1997, p 189; extract from interview with Erica Jong in *Icons, Saints and Divas*, p 24. Reproduced by permission of HarperCollins Publishers.

CHAPTER 4: extract from interview with Erica Jong, *Icons, Saints and Divas*, p 34; extract from interview with Marilyn French, *Icons, Saints and Divas*, p 78. Reproduced by permission of HarperCollins Publishers.

CHAPTER 6: extract from interview with Erica Jong, *Icons, Saints and Divas*, p 33; extract from interview with Erica Jong, *Icons, Saints and Divas*, p 29; extract from interview with Marilyn French, *Icons, Saints and Divas*, p 152; extract from interview with Alice Walker, *Icons, Saints and Divas*, p 212; extract from interview with Gloria Steinem, *Icons, Saints and Divas*, p 134. Reproduced by permission of HarperCollins Publishers.

If you would like more information on Susan Mitchell's workshops, seminars or talks, or would like to offer additional feedback or anecdotes for the next edition of *Be Bold*, please write to:

Susan Mitchell
c/- Curtis Brown Aust. Pty. Ltd.
Box 19
Paddington NSW 2021
Phone (02) 9331 5301
fax (02) 9360 3935
E-mail info@curtis brown.com.au